Max left his little t⌐
way in the world. H
dic student. Many y
was no longer a prob
his old mother. She ₁ooked him over from
head to toe.

"So what happened to your side-locks and beard?"

"Where I live," he said, "if I went around like that everyone would think I was a *greener* just off the boat."

"And you don't keep your head covered. A *cuppel* is too expensive?"

"People like me don't do that any more."

"But your wife, she keeps a Jewish kitchen? Everything kosher? Milk and meat dishes kept separate?"

"It can't be done. The nearest kosher shop is miles away."

"Tell me, you go to *schul* on the Sabbath?"

"If you want to run a business and make a living, you have to work on the Sabbath."

His mother fell silent, rocked from side to side and finally said.

"Maxie, one more thing. Are you still circumcised?"

Are You Still Circumcised?

Are You Still
Creationist?

Are You Still Circumcised?

East End Memories

Harold Rosen

Five Leaves Publications

Are You Still Circumcised?
Published in 1999 by Five Leaves Publications,
PO Box 81, Nottingham NG5 4ER

Published with financial assistance
from East Midlands Arts

east **midlands**
arts
making creative
opportunities

Cover design and typesetting: 4 Sheets Design and Print
Printed in Great Britain by Antony Rowe

Some of these stories first appeared in *Troublesome Boy*,
published by the English and Media Centre.
A Necessary Myth first appeared in *Changing English*.

ISBN 0 907123 48 1

In memory of
my grandson Eddie

For Betty, Michael and Brian

Contents

Introduction
Michael Rosen

As it was my father, Harold Rosen, who introduced me to so many things in life, I must admit it seems peculiar finding myself doing some introducing for him. For many of you reading this he needs no words from me to describe his place as an educator in the field of language and literature. These stories, though, belong to the Harold who grew up in the streets behind the London (now Royal London) Hospital in Whitechapel, London.

For my brother Brian and me, this took place in a doubly mythic time — before we existed and before 'The War'. From the slightly aseptic vantage point of life in Pinner in the London suburbs in the 1950s, our parents gave us glimpses of a community completely different from ours. There was talk of horses falling over on the ice on Commercial Road, bed bugs in tenements and a street that was both the name of a battle and a day to remember — Cable Street.

In my mind as a child, Harold and our mother Connie were messengers from a far-off world where there were *boobas* and *zeiders* and talk of Lenin, *lokshen* soup, Oswald Mosley and *meshuggeners*. People seemed to have longer names then: Gilbovsky, Kesselman, Sokholov and Abramsky. But as this book explores, this wasn't a simple, monochrome picture. No matter how vibrant it seems now, it certainly wasn't cosy. For one thing, there never was before the time of these stories, nor during or since, only one 'Jewish community' or only one way to be left-wing.

As I grew up listening to fragments of the life described in much more detail here, I found myself struggling to understand a complex picture of a way of being. It was at one and the same time working-class, Jewish (but not religious) and Communist. For a while there was part of me which thought no other human beings in the whole world

1

shared these characteristics — apart from our great friends the Kaufmans. Then, bit by bit, over the years, I've learnt how to place us in the world. For a start I discovered that there were others like Harold and Connie's lot to be found in Glasgow and Liverpool, Philadelphia and Paris, New York and Manchester.

Many of these people went through the same struggles to find common ground with people of different backgrounds from their own, in order to make a better life for everyone, just as Harold shows here. So, behind these stories I see the presence of two ideas — a hope for internationalism and a belief in self-pride and one's own culture. I would love to think these two ideas are not contradictory. I don't think in opting for one of these ideas the other should be rejected. Perhaps this book, in part, shows how we can avoid these unnecessary acts of rejection and hang on to both...

...but not in an abstract way. All the people Harold writes about are real. I didn't know many of them apart from his mother, Rose. I remember her well. From my trips to the United States I've had glimpses of her struggling to make a living before the First World War with five children and Harold's father, a blacklisted union organiser. When things didn't work out between them over there she came back to England on her own, bringing the younger children, to the life that Harold describes here. Rose and Zeider, cousin Bernie, Aunt Lally, the teachers at Myrdle Street and Davenport Schools, and the rest, are all part of a very real social world.

And let it be said, however we view the people who chose then and there to be Communists, we should only do so whilst looking at them living their lives in that very real social world and in that specific time. It is a thousand times easier for us now to see the massive gulf between the interests of the old rulers of the Soviet Union and those of the comrades of Whitechapel. If we are ever to get to a place where we can make things better for everyone, just as Harold and his friends and comrades desperately wanted, it will not be in some strange abstract way. It'll always have to start from where people are at.

That's what I love about these stories — they are about where people were at. The ordinary extraordinariness of the people who helped my dear father become the person he is.

I'd like to mention one other delight. Harold read these stories out loud to me as he wrote them. This was a treat both for what they are, but also because his reading recreated those glories in childhood when he would read to us such books as *Great Expectations* and *Little Dorrit*.

May you enjoy these stories as much. *L'chaim!*

Michael Rosen is a broadcaster and writer of books for children and adults.

Comrade Rosie Rosen

I was eleven, sitting on a hard chair, looking at the man across the desk. He looked weary, perhaps even cross. My mother was sitting on a chair next to me. She too was looking across the desk at the man. I thought I could detect the glint of battle in her eye, but the man hadn't noticed. He wasn't looking at either of us but down at the buff-coloured folder which he frowned at while opening it.

We had ended up in this room after crossing Westminster Bridge. From the north side you gaze across the river at County Hall. I had seen it from there several times — a very important building, very governmental, solid, expensive, closed. I had never wondered what went on in it. I don't think I knew that they governed London from there and I certainly didn't know that somewhere in there they governed my education. As we crossed the bridge County Hall expanded, spreading its long façade right along the South Bank of the river. There seemed to be no way into its white coldness. How did anybody get in? Was there a special side door for nobodies? This was not going to be easy. But my mother was not touched by doubt. I could tell by her walk and the hold of her head. She led me round to the back without hesitation. Had she been here before? We went up wide steps into a high entrance hall. Uniformed men asked her business and one gave her directions like a policeman. We trekked up wide staircases into a labyrinth of expensive wood, along panelled corridors, our shoes clacking on polished parquet. We were, I felt sure, in enemy territory. County Hall men and women passed us about their business, intent, silent. I found them sinister.

My mother found the room we wanted. Its ordinariness came as a surprise — drab walls, well-worn lino, a few stacks of files on the floor, books and pamphlets leaning crazily on a set of shelves. A tray of papers on the desk was overspilling a little. I would have liked to be away from there, back on my side of the river, walking freely along the Embankment, taking in boats, bridges, public gardens and saunterers.

The man across the desk looked up and gazed at my mother without saying a word. Teachers do that, I thought. It's how they get on top of you from the word go. My mother wore for the occasion her best black gloves, a newish grey hat and a fox fur. Gloves, hat, fur — she was putting on the style. The man began talking in a rusty voice, affecting infinite patience and civility, cultivated in dealing with the lower orders, especially those from the East End. I heard heavy condescension and controlled insolence. I worried desperately. My scholarship to the grammar school was at stake.

"Before I hear what you have to say, Mrs Rosen, and I shall do, rest assured, you simply must understand I have noted all the details. I have read your letter most carefully. I see from the form you've filled out that you and your husband became U.S. citizens in 1913. I am very sorry to tell you that makes the boy an alien. You won't have read the regulations, of course. Oh, so sorry, you have? Well, they are very clear, aren't they? We are obliged to see that all conditions are met before we can..."

"Just a minute, just a minute. No one has asked me about what happened to my citizenship after I came back to England in 1922. You certainly haven't, have you? I reclaimed my British citizenship in 1924 after they changed the law. There's quite a few things which concern this scholarship which I've not been asked about."

"Mrs Rosen, we have checked the details very thoroughly."

"You haven't got all the details so how can you have checked them?"

At this point she took out of her bag a little sheaf of papers. I marvelled at her composure. The desk-man made an attempt to speak but my mother, certain she had the initiative, cut him off.

6

"No, no. Don't rush me. Are you in a hurry? Let's go through these papers one by one. And you should know that my local councillor, Mr Silver, will be coming to see you and my MP, Mr John Scurr, tells me he'll be writing to you."

The official's manner was changing. Not that he became affable, but he was no longer dismissive and patronising. I had by now shed all my discomfort and sat revelling in my mother's aplomb. I was sure I'd get that scholarship.

I had heard my mother confronting officialdom before — across desks and counters and on our own doorstep. I loved the ways in which she could hold her own with the best of them, just as I winced when I heard nervous old folk struggling for English words to cope with men and their pens and papers and well-timed ways of looking over the tops of their glasses. I admit fully that I thought my mother was something special for all sorts of reasons, some of which don't look very good now. Yes, I know too that mothers are special to their children who are loved by them, defended by them and who are always there. But that's not what I mean at all. I was, I suppose, what I can only call a mother snob, inflated ridiculously by all the ways in which she was different from the Jewish mums who surrounded me. First of all she was born in England, right there in Stepney, not in Minsk, Vilna or Odessa. It followed that she'd been to school in England and after getting a job as a cashier in a large grocer's shop in Aldgate she took extra classes at the People's Palace so she spoke Real English. In the family it sounded Jewish. After all, you can't speak of Passover, a *barmitzvah* or how to make cheese *blintzes* without throwing in a few Yiddish words and phrases and direct translations from Yiddish. But my mother could drop all that very easily and posh up her English when the occasion demanded it. When she sometimes overdid it and made her lips look different my pride went sour on me. Usually I took great pleasure in her sounding so English, believing that it was mostly this which gave her the confidence to cross the frontiers of the ghetto to go to theatres and meetings and to take us on trips into the country. I was pleased she didn't speak to me in Yiddish and I indecently discarded it totally as soon as I could. To me her English made her a cut above, several cuts.

At eight I knew she was the cleverest woman in the world. If not in the world then at least between Gardiners Corner and Burdett Road. I knew, too, that she'd read millions of books — Whitechapel Library was one of her haunts. She had quite a few old books on the shelves of a small battered bookcase in her bedroom, bought, I suppose, for pence from market stalls or in fundraising bazaars. Once I could read I used to puzzle over the titles. So many of them seemed perversely opaque — *Hypatia, Quo Vadis, Pygmalion, Erewhon, Anti-Duhring, The Ragged Trousered Philanthropists* and *King of the Schnorrers.* I had gradually come to the conclusion that she knew every word in the English language. I used to sit on the floor and read when she was in bed in the morning. Once I was struggling through *Robinson Crusoe* because someone had given it to me as a birthday present and because it was brand new with a brilliant red cover, in the middle of which was pasted a picture of Robinson himself bare foot and thatched all over. But inside the print was too small, the black and white illustrations murky and the language elusive. The compensation was that if there was a word I couldn't understand I'd ask my encyclopaedic mother.

"Mum, what's an ague?" (I pronounced it to rhyme with plague.)

"A what? Something wrong there. Read the sentence out to me."

"'I was stricken with an ague.'"

"Ah, I see, you should say ay-goo. It means a fever."

I was seven. I was sitting for the umpteenth time in a large seedy room in Cable Street. A crowd of men and women were sitting on an assortment of battered old

8

chairs under a blue-grey swirl of reeking cigarette and pipe smoke. Against one flaking wall was propped the red banner with a yellow hammer and sickle in the middle of it. Down one end Milly was making lemon tea on an old black stove and serving portions of cheesecake. I was reading *Film Fun* and getting impatient for my mother to get me some of that cheesecake. These were The Comrades at a meeting of The Party in what were always called The Premises. That evening we'd struggled through the damp of Cable Street, across the puddles of the smelly yard and joined The Comrades. I knew in a half-truculent way that there was not going to be much in this for me. From time to time I looked up from my comic and tried to listen to the very serious men and women. Not easy. Each speaker took a long time and there was very little I could understand. Out there, nobody else talked like this, pointing didactic fingers and punching the air. I knew some of them very well for they often came to the house to deliver 'literature' (I had trouble with that word for a long time). When they did, they talked like everyone else — mostly. A few of them gave me their time and joked and told me stories and one of them sang Yiddish songs. Tobias, whom I had heard speaking like an avenging angel, gave me a copy of William Morris's *News from Nowhere* and wrote in it, 'The fault, dear Brutus, lies not in our stars but in ourselves that we are underlings." I couldn't make much of that at the time. Keep it till later, he had said. One day he arrived with a cardboard box full of volumes of an out-of-date encyclopaedia — I think it was Harmsworth's. Volume Seven was missing but we sat together looking at the pictures and he kept up an instructive patter.

"You'll see. Some day this will help you with your studies. It's all in here."

They were shoved higgledy-piggledy in the cupboard on the landing outside my bedroom and I often pulled out a volume and turned the pages. I liked Tobias, even when he was orating at The Premises.

This evening, as usual, the argot which so bewitched them was rolling out. They spoke of the dictatorship of the proletariat, surplus value, the balance of class forces, the crimes of the bourgeoisie. There were dark denunciations of class traitors and deviationists. My mother could speak this language, too. She was at a table at the front of the meeting as Branch Secretary with four other Comrades. After the meeting, long after I had finished my cheesecake and some lemonade, she stayed behind to plan leafleting, a poster parade, canvassing — activities which I'd sometimes be drawn into and be given a placard to hold or a tin to shake. Before The Comrades left The Premises they stopped to take some pamphlets from the piles on the trestle table. My mother took some too. They were as baffling to me as the speeches. They were called things like 'The Final Crisis of Capitalism', 'The Ninth Plenum of the Comintern', 'The Soviet Path to Peace'. I used to look for the ones with pictures in. There were always pictures of men in jail — The Twelve Class War Prisoners (in England), The Meerut Prisoners (in India), Tom Mooney (in the U.S.), marchers with slogan banners, strikers outside their factories and confrontations with police. They became the dominant icons of my childhood and my mother was in the thick of all this. Look at her speaking and them listening. What a woman!

My friends' mothers were not like that, loveable though I found them, plumply installed in their kitchens with their magic recipes, overflowing with affection. They were always good to me, stroked my hair and found me noshy tit-bits. They clearly thought life must be hard for a little boy whose mother was always *schlepping* him to meetings. All the same, if there was trouble with a landlord they were round to our house like a shot.

I was eight and it was May Day, Tuesday morning. My sister and I were standing in a municipal dust-cart. It was a brand new one, gleaming buff paint and the splendour of Stepney's coat of arms on the side. The grand cart-horses were perfectly groomed and their brasses were gleaming. For this day they were decked out with red and yellow ribbons plaited into their manes and tails. Large rosettes bloomed by their ears. There were thirty or so other little children in the cart with us. I looked over the side at the horses' huge bums and twitching ears. How did they know that they must stand still? Why didn't they lumber off down the road? When would the driver come? I couldn't wait. I had a little ache of anxiety about how we were going to find my mother in the milling thousands in Hyde Park. "Silly," said my sister. "Don't you remember last year? We always find her. She comes to get us." So we concentrated on cheering the contingents, passing us with their banners, placards and bands. A fairground was flowing along the street. We were in the dustcart because we were too small to march all the way and our Labour Council, like others, had provided their new carts for the kids and perhaps to add a brave dash of fresh paint for the parade. This was not yet another bitter taking to the streets calling for the release of somebody or hands off something or the end of cuts. This was a street festival, a non-stop party. I was just old enough to know that the tradition then was that you took the May Day holiday, no matter what day it fell on. Workers for Labour Councils were given the day off. I knew too that this was a school day and that we were absentees, a cartload of us. My sister and I started getting at our wurst sandwiches and someone was handing out bottles of pop. The cart moved off and we wore our arms out waving at the folk lining the Whitechapel Road. We sang that we were going to hang somebody or other (Joynson-Hicks, was it?) on the sour apple tree when the revolution comes and hurrah for the Bolshie Boys who didn't care a little bit. Then we entered the hostile silence of the City where gents stood staring stonily. Occasionally one of them raged and shook an umbrella like a man in a cartoon. Safe in our cart we laughed and booed and laughed and jumped up and down.

11

I knew all about May Day. How could I not know? My mother had instructed me over the years.

"They've got their days, plenty of them. Alexandra Day, Armistice Day, Empire Day. And we've got our day, just one, but it's ours. All theirs are for wars, for charity, for showing off with soldiers. They've stuck up their monuments all over the place. Generals and conquerors with soldiers dying like flies all round them and lists of all those poor young men, *nebbich*, killed in their wars. And they always trot out a priest or parson or rabbi to show how holy it all is. We've got our day, our festival, the workers' holiday. It's all ours and nothing to do with them."

She could go on like this for a long time till it became an incantation. In a sort of trance I knew she had to be right. The trouble was I was dazzled by the Lord Mayor's Show and its tableaux and that golden coach. As for soldiers, I wouldn't ever have dared to admit to her that I tingled when they marched by with their shining bands and I didn't know who 'they' were who set up all those days. All the same, May Day in the cart was best, I was sure of that.

The next day I took an absence note to school, nothing very elaborate. 'My son, Harold, was absent from school yesterday because it was May Day, the workers' holiday.' Not a word was said about it and I knew why. The first time my mother had kept me away on a May Day my teacher had grilled me about it. Where had I been? I couldn't bring myself to tell the truth so I became shifty and mumbled nonsense. She lost patience with me and sent me to the Head. It didn't take him long to extract from me that I had been on the May Day demonstration. His eyes bulged and he poked me in the shoulder. He was shouting very close to my face. What could my mother be thinking of? Did I realise that she could be taken to court? Did she think she could keep me away whenever it took her fancy?

As soon as I got home I spilled it all out, especially the poking in the shoulder and being taken to court.

"Court? We'll see about that. And I can tell you he'd better keep his hands off you."

The next day she was up at the school. I wanted to hear every word of what had happened.

"I don't think we'll have any more *mishegas* about May Day again."

"What did he say? What did he say? What about going to court?"

"Court! Don't make me laugh. It wasn't mentioned."

My guess was that Mr Margolis got an earful of Them and Their Days and Us and Our Days. According to her, it all ended up very amicably and by the end she was taking coffee with him like a distinguished visitor. I heard her telling my *zeider* about it amidst laughter.

"We had a nice long talk. Mind you, he nearly took the wind out of my sails. So polite, butter wouldn't melt in his mouth. He says, 'Mrs Rosen, I think there has been a little misunderstanding'. So I think to myself, I know how to manage this. Mustn't push the little man too hard. Best to give a bit of ground for starters. So I say, 'Well, you know, Mr Margolis, maybe I should have dropped you a line beforehand but I thought to myself, a man like you was bound to know it was May Day and, how shall I say, put two and two together.' 'Mrs Rosen,' he says, 'I don't mind saying this to you. I can tell you what it's really about. Truancy in this area is a problem. You've got to watch it like a hawk — helping in the shop, minding the baby, went to my auntie's — you can guess the sort of thing.' Then I tell him why May Day is a different matter altogether. 'Of course,' he says, 'of course.' And this you won't believe, he ends up with, 'Well, we're all socialists nowadays, Mrs Rosen.'" My grandfather slapped his leg, pushed back his glasses and roared. I wondered why they found that so funny. It became part of the family lore, though, and was cited when anyone mentioned Mr Margolis. I knew now I'd have no trouble on future May Days. On this occasion my mother's brief note was meant as a tactful reminder of the negotiations over the coffee cups. As I got older I began to be troubled by the fact that as far as I could tell I was the only one in the school who stayed away. What were the other parents doing about Our Day? You could say that I'm still asking that question.

I was eight still and making my way to school filled with a sick fatalism. There was misery ahead and nothing I could do would stave it off. I was going to Empire Day which the school turned into an all-day jamboree with prayers, hymns, dancing, playlets, readings and above all the grand parade in the playground at the start of the day, to get us in the right frame of mind, We all stomped round in our idea of military marching, a strange little parody, swinging arms, knees up high and feet thumping hard on the asphalt, heads rigid. Small boys and girls in the newest clothes their parents could manage paraded in front of the dull red barrack which towered over them. The five-year-olds, somewhat bemused, got out of step, tripped over each other, and revelled in every second. The tedium and dangers of a routine school day had been declared null and void. All the joy was spiced with competition. Every child brought a Union Jack as they'd been told to do. For days the flags had been on sale in every little sweetshop where they flowered in little tubs next to the front door. If you were really poor you had to be satisfied with a ha'penny one, a pathetic rectangle of thin card glued to a stick with the thickness of a knitting needle. It wasn't going to stand up to a day's waving and jousting but while it was brightly new it could join the colour of the carnival in the morning sunshine. There it would have to stand comparison with those brought by youngsters whose parents could do much better. They arrived with real bunting ones which fluttered properly. There were a few which were taller that the children who held them with golden spikes on top like Prussian helmets. Ostentatious declarations of loyalty, they belonged with the prayers for the Royal Family on the synagogue walls.

On this fine summer's morning I turned grumpily into Myrdle Street, passing the other children flaunting their finery and flags at each other. Not me. I was in my usual

14

old jersey and scuffed shoes and no flag. My mother was not going to have me tainted with the iniquity of Empire and at least one person was going to crack the enamelled surface of unanimity — me. Carefully she had lectured me about what she thought Empire really meant. She had lots of pamphlets on the subject with appalling pictures in them of floggings, shootings and hangings presided over by men in pith helmets. They haunt me to this post-holocaust day. As ever, I only partly understood what she was saying but I approved of all of it. It was my mother saying all this and she knew. She knew the truth about Empire as she knew about everything else, schooled as she was by those Cable Street conclaves. Which was all very well but she had made quite clear that there was going to be no flag for me and no poshing up. It was one thing to be dazzled by her inside knowledge but quite another to be selected as the representative of her principles, defying the British Empire all by myself.

I'd had a taste of this before. Young as I was, I had learned to grit my teeth and stay seated next to my mother in the cinema when, at the end of the show, they played the National Anthem and a picture of King George V was flashed on the screen. All around me seats banged, people jumped up and stiffened their backs. I studied my feet. As they left they glowered and swore at us and sometimes jostled us a bit. I was frightened certainly of being hurt, but the real pain was the sense of isolation and difference. Only my mother, facing them all without a flicker of doubt, stopped me from rushing out in tears.

The martyrdom of Empire Day was going to be quite another thing. I was going to have to bear it all on my own, in broad daylight, amongst my friends, in front of all the teachers, for a long, long day. The anonymous rigid backs in the cinema were nowhere near as fearsome as the prospect of angry, shocked faces in the school yard. I was a small boy approaching the school gate, wanting to turn tail before retribution overtook me. I caught sight of Solly waving a big flag. His father owned an embroidery shop.

15

Lily Kravitz, in a blue velvet dress with a big bow at the back, came running towards me, all friendly as usual.

"My mum says they're going to give us all sweets and an apple each."

"Then she took a close look at me, my flaglessness, my old jersey and my sulky face and ran off to her friends. And there was Monty whose father was always talking to my *zeider* about the affairs of the Tailors and Garment Workers' Union. He had his *shabbas* clothes on all right and he had a flag.

I sneaked into my classroom. My teacher at the time was Miss Waters who was a leg smacker and finger poker. I hadn't been in the room more than a minute or two when I felt her eyeing me strangely. She knew nothing of my mother's little chat with the Head on the subject of May Day. I huddled in my desk amidst the excited children but I couldn't hide from Miss Waters. She made her way towards me and asked me to come to the front of the class. I steeled myself. She whispered in my ear in an unfamiliar, kind voice.

"Harold, didn't you have a ha'penny to buy a flag?"

She had taken one look at my clothes and my misery face and assumed I was too poor to buy even the cheapest flag.

"Here's a ha'penny," she said. "The late bell hasn't gone yet. Nip over the road and buy yourself a flag. For goodness' sake look sharp or we'll be starting without you."

It was a warm, understanding, untypical thing for her to do. That made it harder for me. If I had been given a dressing down or threatened or made to stand in the corner, I might have dug out of myself a little bravado, though I doubt it. I was far too demoralised by now. That sympathetic voice was irresistible. The severe Miss Waters, I felt, understood all my trials and my self-pitying torment. I looked up at her, ready to commit a monstrous betrayal. There was my principled mother quite deliberately sending me to school so that I could make my stand and begin my apprenticeship. And here was I on the brink of betraying her, actually rejoicing at having this hump of anxiety taken off my back. I took Miss Waters ha'penny. She was gently pushing me out of the classroom.

"Hurry," she said. "We'll be waiting for you."

I was away, out of the gates, down the street, across the road and into the sweetshop with its last few ha'penny flags. Mrs Abrams was baffled at my popping up like this. She gave me an old-fashioned look and sold me a flag. I was back at the school and into the classroom like a flash. I imagined the whole class was relieved that I was back in the fold and they no longer had to be sorry for me and Miss Waters smiled at me. She was soon marshalling us out of the building and into the playground. There we were lined up and we peeled off class by class into the march. Some-one had managed to get a piano into the playground and Mr Margolis standing at the keyboard thumped out a mil-itary tune. He was surrounded by the staff who looked happy and approving. As we passed the piano party we waved our flags as we'd been told. Three times round, no less, we went. The relief I had felt soon seeped out of me. And by the time I had done my third renegade waving of that flag I was more downcast than I had been, struggling to do without one. Disconsolate when we finally came to a halt, I did not join in singing 'Land of Hope and Glory', as though I could buy my way back to a clear conscience with this gesture.

I suffered the rest of the day's endless festivities. From time to time Miss Waters took a long look at me, perhaps wondering why her ha'penny hadn't done as much for me as she had hoped. I ate my sweets and apple at playtime, though. I walked home slowly, still holding the accursed flag. I pulled it from its stick and tore it into little pieces and pushed them down a grating in Commercial Road. Then I broke up the stick too, and dropped it into a base-ment in New Road. I sneaked into our house, trying to avoid my mother — not an easy thing to do at the best of times. Soon enough we were in the kitchen together. She scrutinised me with a quick look and said,

17

"What's the matter, son? It was a bit hard, eh?"

She knew what she had let me in for and her voice told me she had had her qualms.

"It sometimes costs to stick up for what you believe in but it's the only way. All the same it was hard for you, wasn't it? I can tell. All day without a flag. That hurt a bit, didn't it?"

Then I did the worst thing possible, the very worst thing.

"Yes," I said, "it did."

Troublesome Boy

Of course, she thought of it. It wouldn't have crossed my mind.

"It would be nice," she said, "a nice thing to do."

"Course," said my sister, "you shouldn't get too big for your boots."

"You don't remember," said my mother. "Why should you remember? I remember."

"What'll I say to him? 'Remember me? The corner near the window. Your favourite pupil. Turns out I'm a genius. My mother thinks you ought to know. How's the little school going? Punishment book filling up nicely?'"

"Such a clever-dick don't need a rehearsal," said my sister.

"Do me a favour," said my mother. "You have to have a bit of consideration. You knock your *kishkas* out for twenty years for a bunch of snotty-nosed *momzeirim* and in the finish what you got to show for it? Pressers, cutters, button-hole makers, market boys. Why shouldn't he know now and then that one of them won his Matric?"

"Passed," I said, "together with thirty other future Nobel prize-winners. Passed. You don't win anything. They give you a nice piece of paper you can nail to the wall."

"*Pish, pish*," said my sister. "*Pish, pish*. Two a penny. It's a nothing."

"He'll go. He'll go," said my mother. "A thank you costs nothing, and you got plenty to thank him for."

"Did I say I wouldn't go?"

My mother brushed the crumbs off the table into the palm of her hand and stood looking at them. She was so full of pride she didn't know where to put it all.

So next day I was off to see Mr Margolis, the Headteacher of the elementary school I'd attended until I was eleven. After five years Mr Margolis had not faded. I had forgotten nothing about him and even now decades and decades later he is more vivid than all my other teachers who are now just fuzzy masks. I don't think there are teachers like that any more, mostly because, thank God, they don't want to be like that and in any case the kids won't let them. Margolis was a monster. A single stony glance from him could set your heart quaking. What am I saying? A glance? Just being there was enough. That silent figure in a classroom doorway could freeze the marrows of forty or more case-hardened little hooligans just by being there. That awesome man could beam his terror across the full width of the Whitechapel Road or from the far end of the playground. If I saw that black trilby a hundred yards away I'd seek out a shop doorway or alleyway to press myself into rather than face the ordeal of simply saying, 'Good morning, sir' and raising my cap (a little ritual drilled to a nicety when you went into the Big Boys at seven). He dressed the part, too. No one I knew wore a black jacket and waistcoat, striped trousers, wing collar and spats. Spats, yes, spats. I used to stare at them, hypnotised, under the iron bar of the oak desk. Little felt-like, ankle high gaiters with an elastic strap which went under his shoe. I wondered what they were for. My mother said it was to keep his feet warm. Though I believed she knew everything, right down to the functions of men's clothing, I felt they were some kind of badge of office. He was the Head and no other teacher wore them. The others wore peat-coloured Harris tweeds, all hairy and pouchy, except for Mr Solomons who wore an immaculate double-breasted blazer and dark grey, pure wool flannels with sharp creases. Very smart, yes, but not what you would call headmasterly. And another thing, the pince-nez. The last exquisite refinement of terror, they enlarged his grey eyes, still and unblinking, to a predatory, basilisk, scrutinising goggle. He haunted my dreams, stalking across vast halls, swishing his cane to winkle me out from a hidey-hole in the cloakroom, contrite and guilty, not of any identifiable crime but of having committed the sin of being. He may have had a wife, and children even. Somewhere, sometime, his face must have thawed into a smile and his voice must have melted into laughter. My fluttering mind could not entertain such an outlandish fiction. Immaculate, he inhabited the brown chipped-tile world of Myrdle Street Elementary School, ruled over it and at nights, roosted immobile in a gruesome eerie, eyes open, probing the darkness for cowering sinners and backsliders.

In those days, the Head sat at one end of the hall, up on a dais, his desk covered in green baize, backed by the Union Jack and portraits of the King and Queen. It seems to me now that he never left that chair behind the desk from which he could hear and see everything. No chance of his not knowing you were late or had managed to persuade a teacher to let you go to the toilet before playtime. Always you had to run the gauntlet of the Gorgon in the chair. On his desk were the cane, the Punishment Book and a large brass handbell. The cane saw regular service and he had a reserve supply pickling in brine in an aquarium under the window. We tried not to look at it during assemblies. All of us would have admitted to anything, served any penance, had he so much as ruffled his brow with a frown. I suppose it was because we would not have paid the price and the bite of pain would not have delivered its moral message. And the Punishment Book would not have recorded your sins for posterity. Turn to any page and you'd have discovered the Moral Order of Myrdle Street School — the crime, the punishment, the executioner's signature:

Disobedience	4 strokes
Lateness	2 strokes
Impertinence	4 strokes
Damage to school property	6 strokes
Talking in class	2 strokes
Foul Language	6 strokes
Obscene Behaviour	6 strokes

It was Obscene Behaviour when Kossoff pissed over the toilet wall.

I still marvel in a dazed sort of way at how much he could achieve through pure, unsullied fear. He taught us for music lessons and we were assembled in rows in front of the piano in the hall. Someone once told me he was a fine musician and he did teach us some good songs. But at that time I had only one musical ambition. I was ten but there were older boys in Standard Seven, some, of course, with breaking voices. Mr Margolis would prowl up and down the rows once he had launched us into 'From the Cotswolds and the Chilterns' (where, for God's sake, were they?) or 'Charlie is my Darling' (Charlie? Could that be right?). Up and down the rows he went, his back bent and his ear cocked, all in the holy cause of hunting down what he called grunters. It was a personal crusade from which he never relaxed. 'Please God,' I used to pray to myself, 'let me not be a grunter. Let me get all my sums wrong, have too many blotty scratchings-out in my compositions, be caught sniggering and whispering, or even trying and failing to piss over the toilet wall.' Yes, even that, rather than being singled out by Mr Margolis, hand-picked inches from his pince-nez and spats and damned as an incurable grunter. Why? In heaven's name, why? All that happened to grunters was that they were sent to the back of the hall where, provided they did not bat an eyelid, they could indulge themselves to their heart's content, listening to the non-grunters' palpitating voices doing 'Nymphs and Shepherds, Come Away'. It was enough for Mr Margolis to indicate that a grunter was a despicable worm and deservedly an outcast for me to dread ending up on the pariahs' bench at the back of the hall. In the army during rifle inspection when the officer of the day fetched up in front of me, about to give my Lee-Enfield the once-over, I caught a whiff of that same kind of dread. But only a whiff.

It was this same terrifying man who pulled about eight or nine of us out of class to prepare us for the scholarship. A couple of boys a year passed and went on to grammar schools. It was a heavy price to pay to have to sit with Mr Margolis and make our mistakes under his very nose. We were supposed to think it a dazzling privilege to be selected and groomed for stardom. My mother, for instance, couldn't contain her delight.

"The Headmaster teaching you. Personally. Better than that *shikker*, O'Carroll."

Mr O'Carroll was in her bad books because it was known that he went to a pub at midday where he probably had a modest pint and a sandwich, so that he became in her eyes that gentile reprobate, a *shikker*, a drunk. He certainly smelled of beer in the afternoons and we used to sing in the playground to the tune of 'Hey Ho Come to the Fair':

Where there's a barrel
There's Jimmy O'Carroll
So hey ho come to the pub.

In fact we quite liked him. But for my mother, the austere and awesome Mr Margolis seemed a much more suitable tutor. I don't know whether he was or wasn't. Perhaps she was very impressed when I told her of one surprising ploy of his. He would give us Latin words and have us try to think up English words derived from them. He'd write up '*scribere, scriptum*' and if we were lucky we'd make a list of scribe, inscribe, describe, subscribe, script, scripture. Someone suggested scribble and he didn't seem quite sure. When it came to the exam there was none of this in it at all. Perhaps my mother hadn't got it right but I passed and that vindicated her completely.

"Without him," she said, "you'd be sitting in Standard Seven for another three years like those other wooden heads."

So I left for the Grammar School and glory and five years later passed the Matriculation exams. To be honest, I didn't think to myself on hearing my results read out, good old Margolis. If it weren't for him, etc, etc. In fact at that particular joyous moment I didn't think about him at all. It was only when my mother started nagging me to go

23

and see him that Mr Margolis came to mind. The truth is I wasn't keen because I just couldn't see us exchanging pleasantries and having a friendly laugh about the good old days and him telling me he knew all along what a brilliant scholar I was and would I remember him to my mother. I knew it wasn't going to be like that but I also couldn't imagine what it would be like. So I felt at best dutiful and distinctly sulky. The thing to do was to get it over as quickly as possible.

Mooching along the road to the school I'd forgotten that I had to get into the place. Those old London three-deckers loomed over the area like Bastilles, designed to resist the barbarian natives who surrounded them. What's more, once they'd got you in you couldn't get out because they locked you in. After the second late bell the caretaker did his rounds and turned his key in the narrow single gates pierced in the high walls. Carved in the stone lintels were the words Infants or Girls or Boys. The iron bars of the gates were covered with a sheet of metal to seal you off from the world outside. To get in after the late bell you had to ring and bring the caretaker from his lair, all wheezes, grumbles and frowns. It was the perfect system for making you tremble with guilt, even before you confronted Mr Margolis' glare. When I had the perfect excuse for being late, like a trip to the dentist's, I couldn't shake off the feeling that I'd done something wrong.

So I walked down Myrdle Street, passed the sweetshop, to the Boys' entrance, a bit disappointed that the turbaned Indian man with his strange little barrow wasn't there any more to sell his tiger nuts, black locust pods, liquorice root, Polish nuts and Indian toffee. I'd have bought some tiger nuts and had a nibble for old time's sake. How quiet that huge school sounded. Somewhere pens were scratching, a child was being ticked off, pages were rustling, chalk was tapping and squealing on a blackboard. A bored boy was probably sitting in my old desk, shuffling his feet. Perhaps Mr Margolis was padding from one classroom door to another, peering through the glass panes. Perhaps a monitor was distributing ink wells or paint pots and was making chinking music. But the great hulk of the school was as quiet as a convent.

I rang the bell. I could hear the lock being fidgeted with and there was the caretaker, looking older and more tired but just as disapproving and testy as ever.

"What do you want?"

"I've come to see Mr Margolis."

"What for?"

Not an easy question really. Words didn't come easily to the triumphant Matriculated scholar, paying his condescending visit. I cursed my mother's insistence.

"I've come to tell him about my exam results."

He looked at me without moving and stayed silent. It was as though I'd said nothing at all.

"Well, I used to be here, in Mr O'Carroll's class."

He made an impatient noise somewhere at the back of his throat.

"Up the stairs, over there. Top floor."

And he was on his way. I couldn't resist saying loudly enough to his back,

"I should know. Went up them often enough, didn't I?"

Some of my cockiness restored, I went up the staircase, passed the Infants on the ground floor (was the beautiful Miss Gwyllym still there, with all that heaped auburn hair?), past the Girls on the first floor where I had never been. Last lap. Might as well be honest. My mind for a second or two toyed with the notion of turning back. The whole enterprise now seemed ludicrous and distasteful. I was even sketching out a tale to tell my mother. 'He wasn't there. Out on business.' or 'He was teaching a class for an absent teacher'.

By now I was at the double doors to the hall. I went through and there he was, at the end of the baize-covered desk, all his accoutrements in their old places, the cane, of course, neatly set out on the table. To the left of him was the glass-fronted cupboard which someone with a nice sense of humour had named The Science Cupboard. The

25

same old mangy bird wing, grey dusty fossils, knobbles of nondescript rock, some bottles with coloured liquids in them, a sloughed snake-skin, a little stuffed rodent, threadbare beyond identification.

The whole length of the hall between him and me. I hadn't got half way and was already out of countenance. I fetched up in front of the dais and the desk, and steeled myself to cope with the pince-nez. Who makes the first move, I wondered. Him, surely. He must greet me in some way or another, if only to ask me my business. By now I didn't quite know what to do with myself. I wanted to put my hands in my pockets and look at the tips of my shoes. I wanted to lean against something or sit down but I knew I shouldn't and couldn't. A silence came down on us and I had no choice throughout but to clench my fists and, unbearably, to look him in the eye. And so I waited and waited and waited. Mr Margolis moved his head very slowly from side to side. Finally he spoke.

"Don't remember the name but a troublesome boy, a troublesome boy."

All the old terrors gripped my guts. I shrivelled to ten-year-old size. Had he ordered me at that moment to put out my hand, mesmerised, I'd have done it. Such is my memory of that moment that I can tell you absolutely nothing about what followed — all, all totally erased from my record.

Kleptomania

I became a thief at eight or nine years old. Up to then I'd gone straight. I don't think I'd stolen a thing. That can't be quite right. I'd taken a cheesecake or two from the larder under the area grating next to the coal or a few Bourbon biscuits on the way back from the grocer's. But they don't count, do they? My *booba* or my mother would not have called it stealing, naughtiness, perhaps. Furthermore, I didn't have any criminal yearnings at the time. I didn't lie in my bed at night plotting little raids on Mrs Abrams' sweetshop nor how to lift a toy from Danziger's. When I found out that Les took money from his mother's purse from time to time — he let it out in a braggart mood — I was horrified. I got a penny a week pocket money but he had a shilling in his hand, twelve weeks' worth at one go. So when I became a thief it was a new way of life, sudden, absorbing, spiced with pure joy. I went on regular expeditions and looked forward to them, even more than going to the pictures at the Rivoli on Saturday afternoons with Solly. I think I am entitled to say that I wasn't so much a thief as a kleptomaniac. I haven't checked that meaning of that behaviour in the psychology books. You look it up and judge for yourself. But maniac I certainly was for a while. I didn't sell what I stole. I didn't show my loot to friends in a secret huddle. I didn't gloat over it privately like the misers in stories, but I stole, passionately, platonically, piously, unreasonably.

Where did I steal from? Not from Spiegelhalter's jewellery shop, I can tell you. Woolworths. Where else? The one at Gardiners Corner. It had opened just recently and for us kids it was pure magic. We wandered round bemused in the midst of the liveried decor. The awe soon wore off, so much so that nicking began and was developed by real dare-devils into a pilfering spree. No one got arrested, clapped into irons and sent to Borstal for a mil-

27

lion years. It was a secret underground club. I heard rumours of it on the grapevine. Then one day Davy came over to me in the playground, stood alongside me and gave me a little nudge.

"Here," he said, "look at this."

Dave wasn't too badly off. His father was a taxi driver who read books between fares and kept a cardboard carton full of them all higgledy-piggledy. Davy had more toys than me, including a clockwork train set. His mother, a solemn, anxious woman, always questioned us closely about where we were going. She was sure that at every street corner dangers waited for us — thugs, crooks, murderers even.

"There's *goyim* out there who'd steal the whites of your eyes and anti-Semites who'd knock you about just for the pleasure it gives them."

"Leave off, leave off, Millie," Mr Taxi would say. "You talk like you're still in Warsaw. So, all the same, where are you two off to?"

"Solly said we could play with his meccano."

We'd tumble out of Davy's house and go to the fun fair to watch grown-ups losing money on fruit machines.

And here was Dave breathing down my ear, Take a look at this. In front of my belly he opened his fist. In the middle of his pudgy hand was a brand new silvery penknife. It shone like a jewel. I reached out to touch it and he closed his fist at once.

"Keep your hands off. *Chup nisht.*"

"Be a sport. Let's have another look."

"You want it? You do, don't you?"

"How many blades?"

"Gimme tuppence for it and you'll find out."

"Where d'you get it? You nicked it. You nicked it. Where from?"

"Woollies. Tuppence."

His mother would have had a fit, certain that Davy would be put away for ever. Anyway, I didn't have tuppence. If I had, I'd have cheerfully parted with it for that

28

shiny little penknife but I was in the ha'penny, at most penny, class. Most of us were. Davy was. He was never going to find a receiver amongst us. Weeks later I saw him sharpening a pencil with it.

Whenever I went into Woolworths I tried to imagine Dave going about his business, reaching out for this and that but I couldn't see it somehow. He was a good boy in class, or good enough. Mr Mitchell never shouted at him or made him kneel, touching the wall with his nose. In the street he backed off our modest hooliganisms, riding a few yards at the back of the coalman's cart, shouting obsceni-ties through Mrs Hamburger's door for taking away our ball, knocking down Ginger. I would stop in front of the counter with penknives and wonder how that good boy Davy had turned himself into a cool *gunuf* who could pull off his crime undetected.

Even when we were used to it there was a unique allure about Woolworths. It was a world away from the stalls along the Mile End Waste which I used to mooch past. They mostly sold stuff which didn't interest me very much, ladies' shoes, nails and screws, attaché cases, pol-ishes and fly-killer sprays. I did like the stall which sold mini-junk piled into a rusty tarnished heap of all things metallic but it was guarded by an unshaven ogre with filthy fingernails. Once when I picked out a military badge he said, 'Run along, sonny,' with the grimace of a child murderer. Wickhams was our one big store but it was as quiet as a church with most of the goods out of sight and sales people who did a ladies-and-gents act. 'Yes, madam. No, madam. Not till September, madam.' Yards and yards of dark mahogany counters and unreal display dummies in ridiculous poses. I wouldn't have dared go in without my mother. Woolworths declared itself to the world in large golden letters against a pillar-box red background. Very brash, very seductive. Inside it was cooled down to a pervasive claret. Even the shop assistants, all young women, wore claret uniforms. Wool-worths was modern. There was nothing like it in the whole of the Whitechapel Road except for the new chromium lettering on Jacobs' shop front.

A few weeks after not buying Davy's penknife for tuppence, I was in the living room trying to shut out the sound of yet another row between my mother and Auntie Zelda about who hadn't paid for something. They had switched into Yiddish to curse the better. My mother kept her end up, of course, but by now I knew just how things were with her, a woman with two kids and no source of income, living off the other adults in that swarming house. As always I crept out and across the road to Solly's place. He wasn't in. So in an aimless zigzag I dragged my feet into New Road, past Dr Sachs' surgery where his vast, unreal St Bernard was on the step as usual, steeped in profound melancholy. On past the Jewish day-nursery with its barred windows and little blue-overalled babies pressed against the bars, snotty-nosed and crying. On past the bakers where I could have bought an enormous piece of bread pudding for a ha'penny but I'd already spent it that morning on sherbet. I got to Whitechapel Road and turned left towards Gardiners Corner. Gardiners Corner! Woolworths! I'd do a turn or two, touching anything I liked in that garden of delights. I started walking properly, past the Foundation School, the Yiddish Theatre, the Salvation Army, the Jewish Reading Room, the old bell foundry, Whitechapel Church and its gravestones and then, under the gold letters, Woolworths.

I made my way over to the counters next to the wall, cheap little tools, some flowery china and then the toys. I found myself standing in front of rows and rows of small scale farmyard animals and farm workers with pitchforks and yokel smocks, railwaymen pushing trolleys, nurses with red crosses, policemen, postmen. I shuffled sideways, scarcely looking at them, to be with my favourites, the soldiers, rank after rank of them, guardsmen, grenadiers, lancers in brilliant colours and plain khaki infantry, mostly frozen in mid-stride with shouldered rifles and some intriguing ones firing from a kneeling or prone position. I always lingered over the two rows of hussars with their cockaded black fur hats. My brother Laurie had signed up for the 11th Hussars when he was sixteen. Who ever heard of a Jewish boy running off to join the army? He ran away from home and lied about his age. He'd already run away from my father in America, worked his way across the Atlantic on a merchant ship and turned up at the already crammed house in Nelson Street. I suppose he must have sized things up and taken a way out. But of all things, the army, and the Cossacks, at that. For my mother it was heartbreak and political shame at the same time. He sent a picture of himself looking heroic in full dress uniform, with his hand on a huge shining sword hilt, festooned with white cord. He had written on the back, 'Show this to Harold and see if he recognises me'. I was thrilled. Idiot. My mother cried over it as she did when we saw him off at Tilbury for India and every time his letters came. We never saw him again.

But the soldiers. They gleamed in front of me. I picked one up, looked at it and put it back. Then another. Then another. I felt electric but calm. Then I picked up one more, a horseguard with a silver helmet, white plume, breastplate and black thigh boots. I held it poised over the counter. I wanted it very badly. The shop assistant was a few yards along. She half turned away as she wrapped something for a customer. An old lady next to me was choosing farm animals and saying to herself, 'Goats. Why no goats? A farm with no goats.' Without any rush, almost dreamily, I moved my arm down to my side and closed my fist over my guardsman. I drifted away and through the store. Exhilarated, I went back home. I carefully wrapped my soldier in a piece of newspaper and put him in my trouser pocket. Later that day my mother said, 'Bella's making liver rissoles. She says you can go over to her place.' I was off to The Buildings, a skinny tenement block fifty yards down the road. The staircase up to Bella Aaronson's top flat always reeked of burnt feathers and discarded guts which came from the slaughtering of chickens in the basement. I tried to hold my breath all the way up. Only something as magnetic as the Aaronsons would have hauled me through the stink. Their tenement was so small you moved around it only by squeezing against the furniture but it was a happy place, full of loud voices and laughter. My mother found a dozen ways of getting me over there when the tensions of our overcrowded house began to boil over. The Aaronsons seemed to cope with their overcrowding quite easily. Bella was my mother's closest friend and fellow Communist. They marched side by side wearing red kerchieves on demonstrations. The family was clever beyond belief. Ezra was already at Cambridge, Josh in the sixth form and Eva in the second form of Raynes Foundation School. Mr Aaronson sat playing the mandolin, inventing things and reading the Marxist classics. Josh was making a wireless. He used to take me to watch him playing rugby. I wished I could live in that feudless home, never mind the stink on the staircase.

So I rushed over to The Buildings. Just before I reached the bottom of the stairs I saw that, where the wall met the pavement, the mortar had fallen away and left a black hole. I knelt down and discovered that my junior hand could just get into it. It was bigger than I expected, a little cave. I took my guardsman out of my pocket, peeled off the newspaper and pushed him into the hole. Then I went on up to the mandolin music and liver rissoles. In bed that night I could see my guardsman safe in his dark quarters. No one in the whole world knew about him except me. The following day I didn't feel the least bit tempted to let anyone into my secret.

A few days later I was in big trouble with Mr Mitchell. My division sums drooped messily down the page and were wrong.

"If you make a nought look like a six, what d'you expect?"

Mr Mitchell was getting ratty. In Practical Drawing the shading on my cone was too furry and in the wrong place. In the afternoon I couldn't remember where Vasco da

Gama had been. There were other lapses. At four o'clock Mr Mitchell said,

"Did you leave your brains at home today? And don't scowl at me. You better pull your socks up, Rosen, or you'll be for it."

Which was sufficiently vague to be full of menace. After tea I headed towards Gardiners Corner and the soldiers, cheering up as I went. I came away with another one but it took longer this time because the young woman behind the counter was too close and looking straight at me. I had to take a couple of turns round the shop before I saw her dealing with a customer. This time I moved fast. The soldier was in my pocket in an instant. I left the shop and went straight back to the hole in the wall, put him beside my guardsman then up I went to Bella. Every few days I made another raid. There was nothing very clever about my tactics, in fact they never varied. I can't see why I was never caught and disgraced.

I kept going back to the hole in the wall and installing the latest recruit. I let my blind fingers touch the hidden soldiers but I never took one out, let alone a handful which I might have furtively played with. I could have risked storing them at home in a shoe box, perhaps, behind the old encyclopedias in the dark cupboard on the landing and then I could have put them on parade on the floor when the house was empty. I could have trusted Solly and we could have played for hours in the gloomy old shed in his back yard behind the shop, where we had made ships from wooden boxes and fenced with cardboard rolls. Solly would have loved it. I don't think I could have tried Davy's huckstering in the playground. I didn't give those possibilities a moment's thought. My soldiers were often in my mind which took me into their burrow and rejoiced in their being there and in the prospect of new recruits. Bliss. My hole was beginning to fill up and I was wondering what to do about it once it was full. I hadn't reached a solution. It didn't cross my mind that I might rest content with my little army. Then one early evening I came back with a kneeling rifleman and as I put him in the hole I knew at once there was something appallingly wrong. I moved my hand about. The hole was empty. Not one left. My heart thumped. I dropped to the pavement and sat with my back to the wall. I put my head on my arms and cried my eyes out. I didn't go up to see Bella and the others. I haven't the faintest idea what I did with my last soldier. It didn't matter. I had given up the whole joyous enterprise.

Mr Old was a never-smiling man who came out from his neck in all directions. His acid-holed brown lab coat made him look like a grocer. Not like the biology teacher who always wore a freshly-laundered and starched white coat like a hospital doctor. I wouldn't be sneering at Mr Old's brown coat if, even at this distance, I didn't still feel spiteful about him. We didn't like each other from the beginning. Yet he should have had a lot going for him. He had his own little manor over the gateway of an old blackened building separate from the main school. It's now listed as an eighteenth century schoolhouse. It's still there, a Bangladeshi Arts Centre. His fiefdom consisted of a laboratory, a preparation room and a classroom which uniquely was a little lecture theatre rising steeply in tiered levels, on each of which was an unbroken length of wooden bench and long oak boards dotted with white inkwells on which we rested our notebooks and carved yet another set of initials. Compared with the single-seater desks in the other classrooms this was a paradise of possibilities for nudging, elbowing, ankle-kicking, note-passing and trafficking. When we arrived for lessons there was a clattering din from our shoes on the wooden floorboards and steps as we rushed for favoured positions near the windows, up the top at the back, at the ends of the rows, but never in the middle. *Schloch*, we called him, a Jewish nickname inherited from the mockery of previous generations (would it be lummox in English?).

At the front of the class down in the well he had his own teak bench with sink and bunsen burner, where he would conduct the demonstration of the day, talking to himself, and we would wait for one of his many cock-ups: the brown ring would not make its mystical appearance, the glowing splint would not burst into flame, the colour of the litmus paper would be dubious. We would cheer and yahoo. Even when all went as planned we would pretend it hadn't. As the wine-coloured permanganate of potash streamed up the beaker, across the top and down the sides as it was supposed to, You can see, he would say, just how the heat is circulating in the water.

"No, no," we would shout. "Where? What heat? It's only making the water red, that's all."

"Stand up, Rosen, say that again."

"Me? Why me? I didn't say a word."

"Take a hundred lines."

The fountain experiment didn't fountain, the dessicator didn't dessicate. When hydrogen sulphide was finally produced in the Kipp's apparatus after several false starts we were supposed to confirm that it smelled liked rotten eggs. Some of the lads pretended that they were overcome with the fumes, groaning on their way to unconsciousness, and one bright spark shouted out, Who farted? Disgusting! Schloch dictated,

"Hydrogen sulphide is a colourless, poisonous gas with a smell like rotten eggs."

"Poisonous!" said the fainters, "poisonous! I'm going to report this!"

"It burns in the air with a lilac flame, forming —"

"Lilac flame? We didn't see any lilac flame. You didn't burn it."

"We'll be doing that in the lab in the fourth year."

"Not me! I'm doing physics next year. No farts in physics." There had been a time when science seemed to me to hold some promise. In a rare moment Schloch had gone off into a monologue about perpetual motion and how scientists had tried for millenia to achieve it and all had failed. I went away and found myself thinking about it. I was stirred and challenged. I sat at home, scribbling

35

and diagramming in my rough notebook. I thought I'd cracked the problem in a simple and elegant manner, all on the basis of one lesson on the apparent loss of weight of bodies in water. It went like this. You'd start with a balance beam and from each end you'd suspend exactly the same weight but one of the weights would be submerged in a beaker of water. It wouldn't stay there because immediately it would rise because of its apparent loss of weight. The beam would tilt. But then it would be equal in weight again and therefore drop into the beaker of water. So the beam would go up and down for ever and ever. On a big enough scale, I reasoned, it could be harnessed for all sorts of purposes, irrigation, for example. I came rushing into the next science lesson.

"Sir, I've done it, I've done it."

Schloch looked baffled.

"Done what?"

"Perpetual motion, sir. I've invented it."

I showed him the sketches in my notebook with their crucial up-and-down arrows and gabbled out my explanation. He took the notebook and studied it with great care, I thought. I was waiting for his praise, of course, but much more for shared excitement. I looked up at his indecipherable face. Then he handed me back my notebook.

"It wouldn't work."

Just that. Nothing more. I might have said, 'Sir, sir, we could rig it up in the lab. Just to see.'

Science in me had taken a terrible wound and begun to die. It never recovered.

I was persuaded that whenever collective insubordination broke out I was the one selected for blame and punishment. Mark said, It's because of your red hair. Sticks out a mile. But he was the only one to agree that I had some sort of case. It soon reached the point where in almost every lesson, after about ten minutes, Schloch would say,

"Rosen, out. Stand under the second lamp on the landing."

God knows how many torturing hours of boredom I spent on that landing and how much of the chemistry syllabus I missed. Schloch and I were soon sworn enemies. There was one Wednesday afternoon when I was playing football for a school team and when I got back my pals, killing themselves with laughter, reported that there'd been a subversive, very noisy huddle at the back of the room, just before the lesson was about to begin. Schloch came in and shouted,

"Rosen, you again. Out, under the second lamp on the landing."

They had all pretended to search for me under the benches.

"Come out of it, Rosen. Mr Old wants a word with you."

When it dawned on him what was afoot his purple fury silenced them. At the next lesson I went up to him, aimiably solicitous.

"Sorry I didn't make it to your last lesson, sir. I hear you were looking for me. I knew you'd miss me."

"Rosen," he said, "any more of your cheek and I'm sending you straight to the Head."

I knew he wouldn't. But that was all a year ahead when I was taller than Schloch and could manage him with words and make him turn from me, speechless. But here in the third year I yearned for revenge. At least I think now that's why I took up the criminal life again in a strictly kleptomaniac style.

The door to the prep room opened onto the penitential landing. It had another door which opened directly into the little lecture theatre. A day came when I decided to risk all and take a look inside. It was, after all, Schloch's lair and strictly private. The handle turned quietly enough and I was in. It was beautiful. One corner was snugly domestic — a small oak desk, on it a pipe and tobacco tin, a college photo of a football team in which I could spot a bright and unwearied Mr Old. His overcoat and gown hung from a couple of clothes hooks on the wall. The curved teacher's chair had a green velvet cushion on the seat and a fine china teapot and tea cup and saucer sat on a wooden tray together with a started packet of biscuits. I don't know what full-time thieves feel when they first soft-foot into a room which still bears the imprints of a living person. But I was for a second or two abashed, ashamed even. This little corner was more human and decent than Schloch had ever seemed in lessons. I could hear the rasp of his voice through the door.

I turned to tip-toe out, and as I did so I took in the rest of the room. There was shelving all round at waist height, littered with a few bunsen burners, clamps, beakers, flasks, test-tube racks, retorts, rusty tripods and rubber tubing — as random as a junk shop. Above the shelving were narrower shelves with bottles, jars and small boxes, everything in perfect order and labelled neatly. I moved towards them. I plucked off a shelf a little brown glass jar labelled 'Iodine' and slid out of the prep room to take up my station under the second lamp. The hour went faster now and from time to time I shook the bottle and listened to the dry little crystals making rustling music. At home I went into the backroom kitchen where there was an open fire by the side of a black oven. When it got dark, I tipped a few of the black iodine crystals into my hands and scattered them on the fire. I knew what was going to happen. A very beautiful violet vapour went up the chimney. In a few days I had burned all my stolen goods. On my next raid I stole some silvery white magnesium strips. I knew about them, too, and set light to them in our back yard when no one was about. They burned with a spectacular, intense flame. This was all strictly fireworks and nothing to do with an enquiring mind. They might just as well have been Guy Fawkes Day sparklers.

There was no turning back now. When I was sent out to the second lamp instead of plodding out with dull resignation I began to tingle with the thought of my next pad round the prep room. There was a limit to the safely combustible substances so I began to diversify by lifting small objects, some wire gauze, a bit of rubber tubing and clips, marble chips, charcoal sticks, zinc turnings, calcite crystals. I even chanced the fragility of a little thistle funnel, delicately pretty. Once I had taken these things away and gone home from school I didn't know what to do with them. I didn't want to keep them, that's for sure. I just threw them away. Wrapped in newspaper they all went into the dustbin, except for the thistle funnel, which I loved for its own sake, I mean my sake. I wrapped it in a bit of rag and kept it in my satchel where, by a miracle, it survived.

About a week later Nat was smouldering alongside me in the playground.

"Dunce. Right in front of the whole class. Dunce. A snivelling little dunce, he called me."

"A what?"

"A snivelling little dunce. That *schmeryl*, he don't know enough chemistry to make salt water for pickled cucumbers."

I was a bit surprised at Nat getting so worked up at a piece of routine abuse from Schloch of all people, who threw his insults around with abandon. We were all inured to being called stupid in different ways by most of our teachers. It went with being a teacher, though there were two or three who seemed to manage very well without it. We were from time to time numbskulls, thickheads, ignoramuses, nincompoops and plain fools. Schloch once called me incorrigible and I went round trying to find out what it meant until a fifth former told me it was just a long word meaning *dumm*. I liked the word and tried to use it when insulting my friends, You're an incorrigible *katzenkop*. Anyway, Nat's grumps were a bit odd.

"Ferric. I just said ferric instead of ferrous."

Must have been more to it than that. It seems funny now because Nat went on to take a degree in chemistry and became an acknowledged expert in the history of plastics. He usually came top in chemistry but Schloch was very even-handed in his abuse, meting it out to good and bad students alike. He knew nothing about pride, at least, not ours.

39

Nat clearly needed cheering up.

"Here, you wanna see something real good?" I said impulsively.

I dug out of my satchel the handful of rag and then pulled out the thistle funnel.

"A thistle funnel. That's from the lab. How d'you get hold of it? Show us."

"Don't *chup*, you'll drop it. Treat it careful."

"You stole it, didn't you? How did you manage to *gunver* a thing like that?"

"It's easy."

I mindlessly opened the floodgates. I spilled out everything, all the secrets of the prep room.

"With a *naar* like that you could steal the *gutgas* off his *tuchas*, the pants off his bum."

"Tell me," said Nat, "what do you do with it all? Nowhere in your house where they wouldn't find it. You collecting for a chemistry set?"

"Chemistry set! I just get rid of it, throw it away."

"What do you take it for then?"

I couldn't answer that really. The question embarrassed me. I had expected him to get some taste of the pure joy of it all. We sat in silence for a bit and then Nat said,

"They could expel you for that. They would, too. And they might even report it to the police. You'd be a criminal."

I took my thistle funnel back and put in my satchel.

"It's a secret, don't forget. Just you and me."

Some hopes! By the next day everyone in the class knew.

"What's on the list today, Al Capone? Concentrated nitric acid?"

"Could you *gunver* for me some Epsom salts or bicarbonate of soda? My father likes them."

Someone did a take-off of Schloch standing in the preparation room, scratching his head and saying, 'I could swear I put that pipette down here. And that jar of flowers of sulphur, where's it gone? Must ask that evil Rosen if he knows anything about it.'

"Here, Rosie, there's a nice little bank just up the road —"

I didn't enjoy the wit very much and it soon died down. Sometime afterwards a few of us were standing by the school gates at four o'clock, larking about, and suddenly Barney said,

"Rosie, get something from the prep room for us."

"Like what?"

"Anything, anything."

They jostled round me. I'd become a kind of mascot or champion. I revelled in it.

"Get something really big."

"Really big?"

"Yeah, like a tripod or clamp."

I was lifted by their confidence in me, not understanding their vicarious and riskless excitement. I went straight to the wooden steps right by us and up to the landing. I was sure there would be no one about at this time of day. Schloch left at four o'clock sharp. I turned off the landing into the lab. I knew I wouldn't find the heavy iron stuff in the prep room and that there was an iron clamp next to each bunsen burner and sink. I grabbed a clamp, concealed it a bit under my blazer and was soon with my pals by the gate. I got all the admiration I could have hoped for. Barney said,

"You should get a prize for *chutzpah*. You've got something to give the old iron man next time he's round."

"Where we gonna put it?" someone said.

It was 'we' now, was it? I put the clamp on the ground and they stood around it. It looked so outrageously conspicuous that I began to get jumpy. The others looked foolish and were also nervy.

"We'll have to get it back," Barney said.

"Who's going?" I asked.

"What a question," said Barney. "You're the only one who'll do it. There's no one there, is there?"

This was much more than I'd bargained for but I could see there was nothing for it. I picked up the clamp. Up the

41

stairs again, trying to stop the boards from creaking, and then on to the landing. My plan was to put the clamp on the landing and flee but I hesitated. At that very instant, Schloch came out of the prep room in his raincoat and shapeless trilby. He stopped. I prayed and prepared to die. One of my aunt's Yiddish curses went through my mind again and again, 'May God's heat melt him into a candle'. But God's heat did no such thing. He came up to me, bristling so fiercely that I thought he was going to punch me. Instead he grabbed me by the lapel and pushed me to the wall.

"That clamp. How did you get hold of it? You not only chatter and misbehave in my lessons but you also steal equipment. Incredible. Speak up. This is a very serious matter. The Head will hear about this and your parents. What have you got to say for yourself? Do you know how much this costs, you nasty little specimen? What's your tale?"

He hadn't let go of my lapel yet.

"Sir," I said, "sir I... we found it."

Schloch, of course, didn't believe a word of it but he was struggling to find some way of countering my lie and extracting a confession. He let go of me and burned.

"Found? Found? Are you mad? Is lab equipment littering the school playground?"

"But sir, sir, we found it by the school gate just downstairs. You can ask the others. We were larking about when we saw it."

"The others, eh? Just larking about. And they chose you, of all people, to bring it back, the honest one."

"Yes, sir, I said I'd bring it back. Couldn't leave it there."

"No, might have got stolen, is that what worried you? You don't like things being stolen from here, do you? We'll get to the bottom of this, you can be sure of that."

He never did, *gott sei dank*. But when we were in the lab sometime afterwards, Schloch sent a trusty to get some litmus paper from the prep room and he said,

42

"Here's the key. Lock the door after you."

As he spoke I imagined he was looking in my direction. I was probably wrong. I hadn't tried the prep door again anyway and I had lost all appetite for its treasures. Believe it or not, I got a distinction in chemistry in the matriculation exam. I didn't know any chemistry but I had learned a textbook by heart, clamps and all.

Not Becoming a Lawyer

I didn't become a lawyer at sixteen. But then I didn't become a trooper in the 11th Hussars either, nor did I become a bagel seller in Hessel Street market, nor a *chazan* in a synagogue. But not becoming a lawyer was something special. To this day part of me is this not becoming a lawyer.

When I got to the grammar school at eleven years of age, I was not, you should understand, in the business of becoming anything. I had done what my mother expected of me, passed the scholarship, as they used to say in those days. I had got the message from her that the scholarship was very, very important.

"You gotta learn when you do this scholarship you can make a different life. Look at your *zeider*. He's a clever man. He reads everything, newspapers, Karl Marx, Zangwill — I don't know what. But what is he? A machinist. At seventy he spends his life bent over a sewing machine. A machinist. Never had a chance to be a Foundation School boy, did he? So he's stuck to that machine like he was glued to it. But you, you could be..."

I looked up.

"I could be what?"

"Well, you work that out later. You do your scholarship, go to the new school, study, get good marks and then you find out. Look at the Michaelson boy, Aaron. He's a Cambridge college boy now."

I still didn't quite understand what was so important. But it didn't matter. If it was important for her, that was good enough for me. I did my stuff and there I was, a scholarship boy. I had a cap with a lovely badge, a new satchel, and books I could take home. I was dazzled by teachers in gowns and the hall with its timbered ceiling and walls. All that for me was achievement enough. As Mrs Warshaw said to me one day when I'd been a bit cheeky, 'And you're supposed to be a psychollege boy!' which showed I'd got somewhere.

So I had no long-term goals. I wasn't limbering up for a long, long course in deferred gratification. In fact, come to think of it, I was more in the business of short-term gratification, like most of the other boy-wonders in my class. Mind you, I'll admit that a handful of them always worked as though someone was standing next to them with a whip. They crouched over their books, shining with diligence like true Talmudic scholars. *Yeshiva bochers*! A touch and they would have been rocking to and fro. Some kind of strange engine drove them on to their passionate devotions. Yet, if my memory serves me right, it wasn't a dream of becoming something really big — a learned rabbi, a writer of books, the owner of a pickle factory, a pioneering psychiatrist, a research chemist. Nor, let me say it, a famous lawyer. They slogged their *kishkas* out because somewhere out there they had picked up on their antennae the message: either you did business, sold and bought, or you bent over your books and studied. It didn't matter which. And what's more, as they handed in their impeccable homework, I don't think they had in their mind's eye the reward of a studio portrait of themselves capped, gowned and clutching a scroll. They were just being blindly virtuous. We were very busy getting by. We had to learn how to cope with Mr Riley's blind furies. He was a grown man with nice white hair and a white moustache but he could gibber with rage and venom just because a snotty-nosed boy got his sums wrong. Perhaps he was punishing us for having become a teacher. That's not what I thought then, of course. I had come to think of his purple-faced tantrums as the way of the world, the same as Mr Llewelyn's acid mockery, Mr Sansom's profound indifference or Mr Lee's magisterial remoteness — and there were all the others. We had to learn them all, to read them sufficiently well to keep to a minimum all the major disasters — detentions, lines, seeing the Head, and, God forbid, the ultimate indignity, the

46

cane. And then time had to be found for larking about with Manny and Sid. I can't remember exactly what we did except that we laughed a lot of the time and did imitations of our teachers. We spent hours playing football with a tennis ball in the playground, knocking the hell out of our shoes. At home we listened to the grown-ups talking forever and forever of the tailoring and the sweat shop guvnors, of politics, strikes, Mosley's Blackshirt invasions and memories of *der heim* in Poland, or Russia, or Lithuania. We walked round the neighbourhood, beating the bounds of the ghetto, up the Whitechapel Road and the Mile End Waste for chips, sarsparilla and the occasional salt-beef sandwich. And we went to the pictures to see *Metropolis, Michael Strogonoff* and *Moby Dick* and the Barrymores in everything at the Rivoli and the Palaseum. Homework we were sure swallowed up all our spare time but somehow we squeezed in a lot of things between homeworks, nothing very improving though.

Perhaps we kept the career thing to ourselves, unnerved by the unemployed on every comer and the tailors on short time, and the *schmutter* trade on its last legs. There were tales of boys who'd left our school with Honours in Matric who were serving in shops or making tea in offices. We tried not to hear such stories, or put their misfortune down to bad luck. Anyway, things would be different by the time we were sixteen.

Perhaps it was talked about in our homes.

"The Stem boy is a medical student at the London Hospital. You should just see him. Looks like a doctor already."

"Doesn't matter what you do, don't go into the tailoring. Slavery. Better be like a *goy* and work on the roads. Furrier, dressmaker, it's all the same."

"I heard from Mrs Feidleman that if you take a little exam same time you take your Matric you can get a good job with the London County Council. Bessie's boy, Mark, did it."

47

"Do me a favour! Stay on till he's sixteen? He can leave at fourteen, fifteen, and get the same lousy job he'd get at sixteen."

"That boy's so clever he could be anything, anything. So what's he talk to me about all of a sudden? Learning to play the saxophone! To play the saxophone!"

Buzz, buzz. Doing Caesar's Gallic Wars (what else?) in Latin when I was fifteen had nothing to do with getting a job. For that matter it didn't seem to me to have anything to do with anything else either. I must say, though, there were for me excellent, disreputable reasons for liking the fact of doing Latin. It made you one with those splendid young *goyim* in the public school stories who shouted *'Cave!'* when a teacher was sighted and whose teachers in Latin class said, 'Construe, Carruthers Minor'. They never, never talked about their careers.

By the time I was fifteen I'd managed to keep my head above water. What more could anyone ask? My end of term reports were almost respectable but when I took them home there'd be a few barbs which would make my mother jumpy. 'Not very assiduous except at irrelevant chatter.'

"Course, 'irrelevant chatter'. You see, big mouth?" said my mother. "Just like your uncle Bernie, so busy putting in your two ha'porth you don't hear nothing."

"But I came fifth in his lousy subject."

"I told you, I told you," she said, half crying. "Trouble with you, you can't listen — to me, or your *zeider*, or your *booba*, not even your teacher. You're gonna end up as a felling hand."

There was usually enough to console her by the time she reached the Head's non-committal 'A reasonable term's work'.

"See?" I said, taking advantage of her doubt. "'Reasonable.' What more could you want?"

But it was clear that all those expert judges of schoolboy genius and talent did not see me as headed for high renown and gilt lettering on the Honours Board. But my mother still nursed her high ambitions and made me decidedly uneasy. So I didn't dwell on it. From my unde-manding point of view I had managed well enough in school exams and was now steeling myself for the Fifth Form and the most important thing in the world, Matric. We all plunged into the preparation and it blotted out the universe. In the midst of all the pathetic swotting and the slightly hysterical threats from teachers ('You'll fail, you dunderhead, if you don't learn the notes on valency!'), Suddenly we took a bit of time out to talk about jobs. I hope you noticed I have just started calling them jobs. Careers! They have careers teachers nowadays, don't they? Our teachers never so much as soiled their lips with the word 'careers'. They behaved as though this was none of their business. We never expected it of them. There was no question of any of them coming up to me in the corri-dor, putting an arm round my shoulder, and saying,

"What are you going to do, old chap? I mean, what are you going in for? Must have thought about it by now. Accountancy? Medicine? Architecture? Civil Service? Er — Law, perhaps?"

I don't think they cared a scrap. What's more, I don't blame them. They had their work cut out getting us through exams. And they knew, as we only sensed, that most of us would end up as clerks in the City less than half a mile away, where they demanded good Matric results from aspiring office boys.

We would get into little huddles by a radiator or in the playground and talk about what we called work, as in homework, schoolwork, bookwork. It was all a matter of plotting and planning to counter the cunning of examiners with our own wiles. Despairing of passing in Chemistry because of a hopeless teacher and an out-of-date textbook, Manny and I pooled our cash and bought a crammers' book, *Littler's School Certificate Chemistry Notes*. We learned it by heart, testing each other out for hours on end. I got a distinction in Chemistry, never having seen most of the substances I wrote about nor conducted, or even observed, any of the experiments. That kind of swotting was full-time work. A nasty smell of anxiety hung in the air and we infected each other with our fears. The evil worm of competition took over our psyches. When Frumkin started saying knowledgeably, 'You gotta know about the differences between Dissenters, Puritans and Protestants' we should have found that very funny: he was an unbarmitzvahd atheist and couldn't have told you the difference between the United Synagogue and the Hassidim. Instead we lost our nerve and shouted that it wasn't on the syllabus. Secretly we knew he was miles ahead of us with his revision and we hated him for it. All the same, better look up the stuff about Dissenters.

From time to time the other kind of work came up — as in factory work, manual work, clerical work. We were very confused and profoundly ignorant. We didn't know what anybody actually did, except in those jobs we didn't want — tailoring and being shop assistants. Ben's brother was the manager of a cinema somewhere in Dalston and used to stand in the foyer in evening dress and control the queues. Bit of a pantomime really. Jacob had an uncle who went from door to door, buying old jewellery.

"What's he do with it?" we wanted to know.

"Sells it, I suppose."

"Makes a mint, I bet."

"He makes a living," said Jacob.

At home my mother was doing her best to make sure that my nose was in my books every waking hour undistracted by Solly and Len playing football in the street and chatting up the girls in front of Gilbovsky's. I stopped going to the boys' club for chess and table tennis, to Victoria Park running track, to the pictures to see Claudette Colbert and Clark Gable, not because I couldn't have spared an hour or two but because any pleasure would have been stained with guilt.

One day Cousin Leslie arrived at the house. This was an event which did not occur very often. Great aunts and uncles, yes. Cousins of all sorts, yes. They were frequent unannounced visitors. No one had a diary to pencil them in. There was no phone to take a call. Suddenly they were on the doorstep. From the cellar my *booba* took pickled herrings, pickled cucumbers, chopped liver, calves' foot jelly, perhaps, and one of the kids was hurried off to the comer shop for Bourbon biscuits. Lemon tea was made. The visitors settled down and spent hours revisiting the past. The kids listened avidly. I remember listening to the tale of my cousin Noah, educated and well-heeled, who became a Special in the General Strike.

"The *momser*," said my *zeider*, "a Special, worse than a blackleg. Next time he came round I told him there on the doorstep to clear off back to Hendon and join the Cossacks. And you know what? You won't believe this. Three years later, by my life so sure, he had to run off to South America. Sarah said he gambled with other people's money. Just right for a strike breaker, eh? A few more pennies for the miners he couldn't stand."

And always the story of deaf Aunt Rifca. In the middle of a rambling account of my great-grandmother's journey from Odessa to Newcastle (she thought she was going to London) Rifca said, 'Don't be silly, he lived with us for twenty years!' This massive non-sequitur was always trotted out from then on when somebody didn't stick to the point.

But here suddenly was Cousin Leslie, something quite different. He was one of those few wealthy relatives who existed on the very fringes of our lives but occasionally one of them would descend on us out of the blue and set the house a-flutter, make us lose confidence in our pickled herrings and our Yiddish and our family legends. Cousin Leslie was already moving along the dark passage into the living room. My sister told me a short while back, when I was talking about these events, that his full name was Leslie Sunshine. I loved that. You'll see why.

Cousin Leslie was a lawyer, more exactly, a solicitor, and he ran his office somewhere near the City. To all of us he was rich, clever, prestigious, could-pass-for-English-gent Cousin Leslie.

None of us could speak like him. He sounded official. And he looked like those *ganzer machers* on the platform on Speech Day. He was shiny bald, plump in the face, wore gold-rimmed specs and a beautifully cut, perfect suit (if we knew how to judge anything it was how to judge a suit) and he smiled out of it all the time. He went round being nice to everyone. At one point he came over to me.

"You got a scholarship to Grammar School, didn't you? Must be in your Matric year by now, am I right? What subjects are you taking? What's your favourite subject? Do you get good marks?"

Don't ask me what I answered. I was over-awed and I mumbled. By this time my mother had inserted herself behind his left ear. He turned to her now.

"Ah, Rose" (no one ever called her Rose: she was Rosie to the family), "I hear the boy's in his Matric year, eh? How's he doing, would you say? Going to get good results?"

"He's a scholar," said my mother, with a conviction on that score that I had never heard before.

"What more could you want? If he's a scholar he's going to get good results. Tell me now, what's he going to do? You must put your mind to that, you know. No use leaving it to the last moment. You've got to weigh up the possibilities. Have you thought about that?"

"He could stay on," my mother said, but did not sound very convinced herself. Small wonder. I hadn't heard a word about this possibility.

"Mmmmm," said Cousin Leslie, as though my mother had said something implausible, perhaps even silly. "Have you thought about Law, Rose?"

"Well, no. Not Law. No, I haven't. Nor have you," she said, turning to me. "You haven't thought about Law either, have you? Not Law."

All those Jewish jokes about my son, the lawyer! I had already heard and even told a few. But this was getting serious. What exactly was Cousin Leslie getting at? I knew that in those days you had to be articled to someone in a practice, a sort of posh apprenticeship, and you paid a lot for the privilege. If Cousin Leslie was making this proposal, he also knew we didn't have a penny.

"Listen," he said to me again. "When you get your results — that's in August, isn't it? — if they're good, something better than a row of bare passes, get in touch with me. Do you understand? You'll find me in the phone book, Rose."

He was gone soon after. My mother and I looked at each other. I was overjoyed, excited and a bit confused.

"You know what he means, don't you? Does he have to write it on a piece of paper for you? He's a man of few words. He'll take you on and we won't have to pay. Nothing. You're going to be a lawyer. Just get your Matric and that's it."

Cousin Leslie Sunshine had worked a miracle. I could get back to my books with my future settled. It was, I felt, a decidedly grand one. I hadn't had to lift a finger and I was almost a lawyer already. What did a solicitor do? What would I be doing to start with? I hadn't the faintest idea and I didn't give a damn.

Don't think I went back to school and bragged about it. There are unwritten rules about such things. All the same, at those rare moments when our chatter turned to jobs, I'd drop into the conversation that I was going to become a lawyer. At first they only half believed me, if at all.

"A lawyer," said Clever-Dick Monty, "you've got my custom already for when I take up a life of crime. Mind you, I don't think you look the part with all that red hair and bad jokes. Anyway, where's the money going to come from?"

But they came round soon enough and it gradually became part of the wisdom of the group that Rosen was going to become a lawyer just like Manny was going to do science. It felt very good, even better than doing Latin.

I said before that our teachers never showed the least interest in what we might be doing after we left their care but there was one exceptional occasion. One day when the exams were terrifyingly near our Form Master, Mr Lee, came into the room with a large official sheet of paper.

"Now," he said, "I've been asked by the Head to fill in this form which will give him details of what you propose to do after completing your matriculation examinations." Hands shot up all over the place.

"What if you don't know, sir?"

"I haven't made my mind up, sir."

"Depends on the results, sir," said Reuben. "Doesn't make sense." Chancing his arm he added, "What's the Head going to do with it all, sir?"

Mr Lee raised his hand.

"Common sense has gone out of the window here today."

We pretended to look for it, craning our necks.

"And good manners," said Mr. Lee. "It's very simple. If you know, say so. If you don't know, say so. If you are not sure, say something like, 'Possibly this or that'. Is that clear?"

Reuben whispered noisily to me that if we didn't know what they were doing this for we shouldn't say a word. He was always red hot on civil liberties — in principle.

"Reuben," said Mr Lee, "if you find all that too much for your brain to take, you can have a private consultation at the end of this lesson."

Reuben, who'd had a good run for his money, subsided irritably into his desk.

Mr Lee went through the class list.

"Abrams, Berkoff, Cohen, Cemowitz, Dolinsky, Danziger, Frumkin, Friedman, Greenspan..." There were a lot of not sures and a few surprises. Someone said he was going to Regent Street Polytechnic (to do what? why hadn't he said?). Levin said he was going to stay on in the Sixth Form which made Mr Lee look over his glasses for a long few seconds. My turn came.

"Law," I said, loudly and boldly. Mr Lee pretended he had not heard.

"Law," I repeated, staying calm.

"Keeping it or breaking it?" he asked.

The arse-lickers fell about. My friends gently hissed. Later in the playground, I must admit, there was quite a group who were chanting, 'Keeping it or breaking it? Keeping it or breaking it?'

It was all over and forgotten soon enough and it was back to exams. I sweated with the others through the sweltering July days. I joined the post-mortems after each paper.

"Bloody swindlers! No question on the Factory Acts."

"But Schloch said there'd be no question on bromine."

"What did you get for question seven?"

I had my worst moment in Algebra. I put my pen down in despair and listened to a barrel organ in the street below playing the Valeta, a tune my mother loved to dance to. Soothed, I went back to the paper and found it more doable than before. Everyone who's ever taken an exam knows all this and still has nightmares about it.

August came and we assembled in the hall to hear our results. I'd done it. Some distinctions, some scrapes. I'd got a decent Matric. I was going to be a lawyer. I rushed home with the news. My mother did not hesitate.

"Phone Leslie. Phone Leslie. Now. Here's the number."

She pushed some coppers and a scrap of paper into my hand. I ran to the kiosk outside the Sussex Steam Laundry and stood getting my breath back and carefully rehearsed my words. I dialled. It was a secretary.

"Can I speak to Mr Sunshine, please?"

"Who's calling?"

"Tell him it's Harold. I'm his cousin."

She brought him to the phone.

"It's me, Harold, Leslie. I've done it. My Matric. I've passed it. I've just heard, up at the school."

"Yes," he said. He sounded a little puzzled and not particularly pleased. I stumbled on.

"You remember? You told me to get in touch. To let you know if I got my Matric. I mean if I got good results. Well, I did. Shall I tell them to you?"

"Not just now. Some other time. I'm glad you did well. Very impressive. Rose must be absolutely delighted. Congratulations and good luck."

And Cousin Leslie Sunshine put the phone down on me. For ever.

Cribs

I was sitting there so bored I could have cried. I'd finished the arithmetic paper and was waiting for Mr Powell to declare the exam over and done with. Following the order of the time, if you finished before the Head rang the bell in the hall, you sat there in total silence doing nothing. Could have let us have a book from the cupboard, I thought. Like *King of the Golden River* which we'd started reading in class, and which was nice to handle, bright red and gilt lettering. It was all good practice for something or other — the army? prison? — but an excruciating strain for a ten-year-old. All you could do was look round the room to see how the others were making out or study the flaking map of the world and the faded pictures, ' When did you last see your father?', 'The Fighting Temeraire' and 'Napoleon on the Bellerophon'. Most of the others had their arms curled round their papers and their heads almost buried inside them. This was to stop someone nearby from cheating. Bit of a laugh in Benjy's case. He would be lucky to get a couple of sums right and he would certainly not finish more than a quarter of the paper. Yet there he was like a miser over his hoard. He might not be very good at arithmetic but he had mastered the ethics of scholarly behaviour. I think he believed that if he only adopted the correct physical posture he would join the elect. Getting sums wrong shows a certain lack of fibre but cheating we all knew was a moral disorder of a much more reprehensible kind. We knew this, not because we were able to take in all that moral business but because we could tell from the scale of the outrage of our teachers when confronted by some protesting little cheat that copying an answer from someone else's paper or writing something in the palm of your hand or smuggling in a tiny scrap of paper was a crime against the social fabric itself. 'Cheating is a kind of stealing,' said Mr Powell. 'It's stealing knowledge'. Dicky Kahn thought that was funny. 'So *mein kind*', he said later in a Yiddishe momma's voice, 'you mustn't be a knowledge *gunuf*. Same as in Woolworth's, *tatele*.'

In the morning assembly after a suitable run-up of prayers and a hymn, Mr Margolis has sketched out the ground rules.

"Tomorrow you all start your exams. This will be the most important day of the year. You will be given full instructions by your teachers but I want to say something special to you. As you all know, if you copy or even try to copy from another boy's paper, that is cheating. All your work must be your own. Never try to ask someone else for an answer and don't attempt to give one. Anyone doing any of these things will be severely punished."

Some of us glanced at the canes in brine in the aquarium. Mr Margolis had used one of his special voices, not the more-in-sorrow-than-in-anger one, not the bespoke sarcastic one for a shaking criminal hauled to the front of the hall, but the high solemn one of an Old Testament prophet warning of a plague or the risk of God's displeasure. I can't say I was following very closely. One way to avoid getting shaky and afraid was not to listen. In any case I didn't think any of this concerned me very much. Cheating wasn't my particular line of crime. Mr Margolis was now taking one of his long pauses. His gaze went to and fro and through us to let the dire threat sink in. And then he started up again.

"Now when you're doing your exams you'll stay out of trouble if you keep your eyes on your papers and don't look to right or left. Like that idiot at the back is doing right now. Yes, you with the uncombed hair."

And here he suddenly bellowed,

"Get out! Get out of my sight! On the landing. I'll deal with you later."

The uncombed one, for us a hero, a martyr, slouched out.

"You see?" he went on, "there's always one. Make sure it isn't you. Another thing. You mustn't make signs of any

58

kind to another boy. Don't pull silly faces. Don't make lip movements. Don't signal with your hands. It's all cheating. Cheating, you understand. We are not going to tolerate any of it. Not a flicker of it. There will be no cheats in my school."

Now that I'd finished the paper there was certainly no need for me to cheat from the arm-curlers around me. Then I noticed Dickie Kahn. He was just across the aisle from me and he too had finished. He was leaning back in his seat, arms behind his neck, and staring at the ceiling. I tried to catch his eye and failed. That was a risky thing to do. All classes in the Big Boys were examined at the same time. The classroom doors were fastened wide open so that Mr Margolis could monitor the whole exercise from the hall and prowl round the classes to root out the slightest irregularity and in particular, cheating. The open doors were also to impress upon us that this was one of the big ritual moments of the year. They also made us feel more exposed, out in the open. Given the surveillance of our own teachers they would otherwise have seemed foolishly unnecessary. All in all, by the time we'd started examinations only wild desperation or advanced idiocy would have made anyone try it on.

I looked across at Dickie Kahn. This time I did catch his eye. Catching an eye was, I suppose, within the meaning of the act. But I did. And he let the faintest hint of a smile cross his face. There were just a few minutes to go. He silently mouthed the word, 'Finished?' I mimed the answer, 'Hours ago'. As I did so, a great terrifying shout hit my ear like a punch. It was Mr Margolis who had spied me from the open door, rushed in and bellowed into my ear, 'Cheat! You were cheating! Mr Powell, this boy was openly cheating. Now, cheat, get out and stand in front of my desk in the hall. We know what we do with cheats here.' He was dragging me from my desk and pushing me to the door, past Mr Powell who looked a bit upset. Possessively, he didn't like one of his pupils in big trouble.

Mr Margolis made short work of me. My fear and sense of huge injustice had already set me crying and I made one spluttering attempt at a protest. Much good it did me. Out came the cane and I got two fierce whacks on each hand. Mr Margolis led me back to my class and the others took in my tears and misery. He led me right up to my desk. There was the arithmetic paper I had finished with such assurance. With a red pencil he scored a punitive diagonal line across one page after another and then he wrote on the first page, '0 marks. CHEATING'. I'd been in some scrapes before but nothing like this. And there was worse to come. Every one of the papers I had already done was given a nought mark and I came bottom of the class when minutes before I had thought that Dickie and I were competing to be top. The disaster darkened my world. I had in a way bought the cheating thing and had come to believe there was something despicable about it. But now a thousand Mr Margolises would never convince me that justice had been done and been seen to be done. Mr Margolis had devoured and digested me and it had nothing to do with cheating as I had really understood it. He was the fraud and cheat.

Now there was my mother to face. As I crept home I realised there was no need to assume that she would see me as a branded outcast. She was more likely to worry about my being entered in a dossier somewhere and that the word 'cheat' against my name would dog me for the rest of my days. She had, with some reason, views about dossiers. My best hope was that her view of what she called The System would make her furious about my treatment. System or no System, she was inclined to side with teachers when I grumbled about them.

"That Powell, he never explains properly. He mumbles out of the window and you can't hear a word so I can't do my decimals and always get the dots in the wrong place."

"You know something? Maybe he don't explain all that good or maybe someone else sometimes looks out of the window or fools around with Manny and doesn't pay attention. If I went up to the school and asked how come you don't know decimals, I might hear a thing or two wouldn't make you seem so hard done by."

"Did I say anything about going up to school? You'll make me look like a real mummy's boy. You'll make me look like a real fool."

"I don't have to try. You're making a good job of that without my help."

The matter was left there and she made it very clear that there was no future in spilling out all my little grievances. But if she sniffed out some real injustice she'd be up at the school like a shot. She had already had one or two brushes with Mr Margolis and he'd learned to treat her with care, almost deference.

"Who does he think he is? God? He can make himself a *ganzer macher* with little kids but as far as I'm concerned he's just a tin-pot bully. You see, he's part of The System. He has to teach you to obey, to do what you're told, no questions asked. You know why? Because that's what you're supposed to do for the rest of your life, be a *stummer* little *tuchas-lecher*. Very nice for the bosses. Don't worry, I'll have a word or two with him."

A word or two! I hugged myself. What I would have given to have heard her with a word or two, teaching Mr Margolis about The System. And then I had to remember that when it suited her turn the tin-pot bully was a stern wise man, a *malamed*. And then it was, 'He's got letters after his name, you know that? BSc. That's a degree from a university. It means he's a scientist. You can learn a thing or two from a man like that'.

Out tumbled my story as soon as I got home and I cried again for a bit.

"Enough, enough," she said with her arm round me. "Sometimes I think he's a bit touched, screaming his head off and hitting little boys. Other times I think he just pretends to go mad like that because he thinks the kids might all run wild like little gangsters. Mind you, he'd no business to hit you with the stick just for moving your lips. It's

61

like it was for the Jews in the Tzar's army. Hurting and hitting is no way for a school. Or, come to that, for a man who's been to college."

"What about my marks and making me bottom?"

"Your marks, your marks." She was miles away, talking to herself.

"Bottom, he's making me bottom! He's the cheat, not me!"

"I'll speak to him," she said quietly. "Wash your face and go make yourself a *platzel* and cream cheese."

She spoke to him. I got all my marks, even the arithmetic. The cane she could not take back. As for cheating, I'd begun to think about it.

When it came to it I chose to do Latin. At the beginning of the third year we all had to start on German. They gave you a short dose, three weeks with Mr Jones and *Deutches Leben* and then they asked you if you wanted to continue or do Latin instead. A choice! Every other subject in the curriculum had fallen upon us like acts of God. No one had asked at the beginning of the first year whether we fancied five years' worth of French or a similar sentence of doing chemistry with bloody-minded Mr Old. It was strictly *table d'hôte*. Faced with this new phenomenon, choice, we could have done with a little advice. Not a word. At other schools there would have been some parents who knew about such things or thought they did. Our parents together could have mustered a lot of languages, Yiddish, Russian, Polish, Lithuanian and the men could all read Hebrew. It wouldn't have struck us that this qualified them to tell us about German and Latin. All their languages were part of their incurable immigrant backwardness, usually spoken because they couldn't speak English or couldn't speak it very well or just weren't comfortable with it. As for Hebrew which they didn't speak, they read it because that's how you practised your religion. That's how they learnt their prayers and were able to get to grips with the *Torah* and the *Talmud*. German and Latin we knew were something quite different, real languages with textbooks, declensions and conjugations and you could do them for Matric. The teachers could have said a word or two but they didn't. They certainly didn't compete for our custom. Our own folk-lore had it that lawyers and doctors needed Latin though no one seemed to know why. We knew that you didn't learn Latin so that you could go and speak it to the Latins. And Latin used to happen in the school stories we read. None of that mattered very much to me. I was plumping for Latin.

It was like this. English was the language spoken in my house. All the adults could speak Yiddish fluently but they only used it when they didn't want the children to understand or when people came to the house who were only at home in Yiddish — which was most of them. The English spoken was peppered with Yiddish words, exclamations, curses, threats, proverbs. Their English had occasional touches of Yiddish grammar and was usually spoken with a distinctive Yiddish lilt. They sang Yiddish lullabies and folk songs, '*Herrt a meisser, kindele*', '*Az der rebbe Eli Meli ist gevoren sehr gefreli*'. I picked up a lot of Yiddish this way and would not have spoken it at all if it weren't for the fact that in the homes of all my friends Yiddish was the language you lived in. Simply to be civil, say 'please' and 'thank you', 'good Sabbath', 'Is Solly in?' I had to muster some working Yiddish. I was never really fluent with it but all my school friends could speak it as confidently as they spoke English and they usually spoke to their parents in it. There was even Manny's father who, as a Jewish socialist, was militant about Yiddish. 'Forget Hebrew,' he would say, 'it's for the Zionists. Yiddish is the language of the Jewish proletariat.' As a member of the Bund he sent Manny to evening classes at the Workers' Circle where a scholarly little man introduced him to the Yiddish literary canon. Sholem Aleichem, Y.L. Peretz, Sholom Asch and the rest.

Neither I nor my classmates would have known that Yiddish began as a mediaeval German dialect. It was only when

63

we began our classes that it dawned on us that German sounded very familiar. The fluent Yiddish speakers were cock-a-hoop. If only French had been like this. As Nat said, 'German's only posh Yiddish'. Whole sentences and dozens of words were understood immediately. They all took to German like ducks to water. Mr Jones couldn't go fast enough for them. But my nose was out of joint. I was floundering. It is Latin for me, I thought. At least we'll all start level pegging. So eight of us went down the corridor to the Sixth Form Library, all oak panels and glass-fronted book cabinets. We were an elite before we'd started.

Mr Chester, the Latin master, was a bit remote but quite a gentle man. With only eight of us to teach he relaxed all the disciplinary ploys. No one was given lines nor detentions, nor made the butt of sarcasms and savageries. We were a cosy little club. And Latin wasn't difficult at all. You didn't have to try to speak it. Once you had galloped through all the conjugations and declensions you translated simple little phony sentences about Lucius, the line of battle, centurions and Gaul. Then you progressed to concocted little paragraphs mostly military or mythological. At the beginning of the Fourth Year our happy little band were in for a bit of a shock. We had Virgil's *Aeneid*, Book Two, the Trojan Horse one, thrown at us and we suddenly felt we knew no Latin at all. You had to prepare a chunk at home the night before a lesson. It was slow work. The standard little blue edition of the time had a driblet of Virgil's text wedged between an Introduction and the Notes and Glossary. I pored over the pages, fluttering to and fro, in an effort to drag some kind of meaning from them. All very rabbinical. Back in the class the ancient method persisted. You took it in turns to translate a ration of lines. Latin had become a wearisome grind. Mr Chester, with no recriminations, would patiently help out if you got stuck but there was no joy in it at all.

Then the word went round that if you went to Foyles in the Charing Cross Road you could buy an English translation of Book Two, quite cheap as well.

"It's what's called a crib," Simon Frumkin said with authority.

"A crib?" I asked. "Funny word."

"It's a book to cheat with, *schmeryl*."

So we elected him our book buyer and he came back from Foyles with a clutch of these so-called cribs. I took my copy and went off to a quiet corner to examine it. I took an immediate dislike to it. It looked and felt as though it had been printed on thin blotting paper. There wasn't very much of it. The text had been crammed into almost all of the available space on the page and the print was microscopic and slightly fuzzy. Nothing broke up the unrelieved tedium of the pages. There was only the identification at the top of page one, Classical Translations No. 27, *Aeneid* Book 2, B L Braithwaite, BA. If ever you wanted to make a publication look like under-the-desk contraband, this was it. The translation was in an English which had been tortured to enable desperate learners to match phrase with phrase. My disgust did not prevent me from using it though I never took it into class out of a kind of squeamishness I didn't know I had in me. I certainly didn't want Mr Chester to catch me with anything so obviously grubby, without the slightest pretence of being a real book and manifestly designed as a swindle. I mustn't overdo my distaste, though. That crib saved me hours and hours of slavery. High-minded principles were not going to stand in my way.

Then one day I was in Whitechapel Library. It was one of those magnificent Carnegie libraries which the old London Boroughs prided themselves on. Its stock was as good as a university for many people in the East End. I didn't know my way around the shelves all that well. I usually headed for the novels and, less often, a book to help me with my homework. Tentatively, I had picked up *All Quiet on the Western Front* and *Brave New World* which an English teacher had suggested and I'd toyed with Trevelyan's *History* but, glancing at a few pages, I could see it was over my head. I was wandering past some unfamiliar shelves when I spotted a large handsome collection of many books. I could see there were really two collections in the same format, one bound in green and the other in red. I went closer and read their titles. Here, I realised, were the classics, all of them, Greek in green, Latin in red. I looked along the Latin shelves and there was Virgil's *Aeneid*. I loved the feel and look of it, good paper and friendly type-face. It had class. I saw it as coming from a world where fastidious gentlemen sat in leather armchairs and read it easily and earnestly. Flicking through the pages, I realised there was something unusual about the book. I had no idea such books existed. On the right-hand page there was the Latin text and on the left an English translation. I hunted for Book Two and for the bit I had just been working on, Anchises being carried from burning Troy. The translator, I could see even then, had been free and easy, making his prose read like a real English book. I stood and read a page or two, savouring it. I had stumbled on the Loeb Classics.

I took the book out and went home. I flung Braithwaite into a corner, planning from then on to work only with my find. I wish I could say that I was a really generous-minded youth and immediately shared my find with the other founder members of the Latin club. I didn't let the thought cross my mind. It was my own discovery and besides, they were satisfied with their grimy cribs. They'd find out soon enough anyway because I was going to take my treasure quite openly to the Latin class. Mr Chester, I was sure, would be pleased and perhaps impressed.

It came my turn to translate. I took my book from my satchel, placed it on the desk and began glancing from time to time at it and my own notebook, I had scarcely translated two lines when Mr Chester stopped me.

"Rosen, what have you got there?" He sounded quite surprised.

"A translation I have been using, sir," I said chirpily. Mr Chester was looking genuinely baffled and, I thought, a little hurt.

"You know that's a crib. You not only bring a crib into class but you open it under my very nose. Don't you think that's a bit silly?

"But, sir, this isn't a crib. This is a Loeb Classic." I said 'Loeb Classic' as others might have talked of the Seven Wonders of the World. Mr Chester smiled and nearly laughed.

"Rosen, if you bring a Loeb Classic to class it becomes a crib. There's no difference at all."

He picked up my book and read a bit to himself.

"Fine translation. Don't bring it to class again, there's a good lad."

The club members bunched round me after class. They weren't angry or jealous. They just wanted to thumb the book and enjoy it a bit. After that they always came to me to copy out the next passage. But I felt cheated.

Whenever I went past the Mission to the Jews in Philpot street I thought of Gothic. I mean the Gothic language. I first encountered Gothic as soon as I went to the University. Like most people I had never heard of it before and I've heard almost nothing of it ever since. It doesn't exactly crop up. Somebody had decided that if you were to get a degree in English Language and Literature then you simply had to study Gothic. On the face of it the connection between the two was not too obvious to an eighteen-year-old. I suppose that tucked away in some dusty archive in the Senate House there is a solemn rationale for this bizarre element in our course. The main thing is that Gothic is the earliest Germanic language known to the trade and no doubt there were scholars who got very excited about this. It's a bit like those people who get quite a buzz out of tracing their ancestors back to the Normans. Perhaps there was a lot more to it than that but I had expected university English to be one long round of delight and professors talking like Quiller Couch and Leslie Stephen and endless days reading novels and poems and plays. But here on my timetable was Gothic (to say nothing of Anglo-Saxon, Phonetics and Palaeography) on Monday mornings at 10 a.m. with Dr Brookfield.

I had been far too naive to investigate beforehand what English actually meant at university, and when I discovered it meant Gothic, that was a nasty shock. I went off to buy my Gothic textbook in a rebellious frame of mind. Page after disheartening page of Gothic grammar which I discovered very soon was mostly invented on the basis of some identikit principles which I never fully understood. The grammar book had asterisks against the word forms they had made up. Most of the words had asterisks against them. I took it to the first class with Dr Brookfield. She was a frail-looking oldish lady with a chalky white face and wire-wool hair. She always wore a navy-blue dress with a white lace collar and round her neck was a large ornate gold cross. We soon found that she was an amiable lady though as a mentor she might have been made of steel. I remember that in her first hour with us she told us we were going to study a Gothic text by someone with the unlikely name of Ulfilas. We'd find it at the back of our text book. This Ulfilas had translated the Bible into Gothic in the fourth century AD. It turned out that only a few tiny bits and pieces of Ulfilas's mighty work had survived and some of this is what we had to prepare for translation in class. So this was going to be our dry bread and water for the year and the price we had to pay for enjoying ourselves with Chaucer and Shakespeare was a fictional grammar and old scraps of the Bible in an utterly outlandish language.

Then Dr Brookfield suggested that we should all toddle off to the British Museum just down the road to take a look at Franks Casket. That had a nice homely ring. It turned out to be a decorated box with runic inscriptions all round it. We didn't know why Dr Brookfield had told us to go and look at it. Maybe Mr Ulfilas wrote in runes. Were there quotes from him on it? Was it a casket from Gothic times made in Gothic-land? Why was it called Franks Casket? Was it made by Frank or for the Franks? I found in a corner of the display case a puzzling translation of the runes and enjoyed an indecisive bit which read, 'The whale became sad (or, The ocean became turbid)'. The scholars didn't seem too sure about their precious Gothic. After all, there's quite a difference between an ocean and a whale. Dr Brookfield never mentioned Franks Casket again. She might just as well have sent us to look at the Rosetta Stone. Perhaps she knew how baffled and dismayed we were by the prospect of the Monday Gothic hour and thought a pretty little ivory casket with carvings of the Adoration of the Magi and Wayland the Smith on it might cheer us up. Doesn't seem likely. After I'd been in the college a few months I'd got to know the very popular beadle in the cloisters in his claret frock coat and gold-braided topper. His name was Frank. I said one day.

"You know, Frank, your name's in the British Museum. They've named a box after you."

"Have they now? A student told me that when I came here in 1928 and I said, 'Listen, Sonny Jim, Frank's a very common name but you can keep your comic turns for your clever pals' I may be wearing a funny hat but I'm not a museum piece yet."

Back in our class we were soon on the treadmill, preparing and translating the fragments of Ulfilas. The first year English group, it must be said, consisted mostly of young women who came in from the outer suburbs each day. They were clever, very diligent and almost always unquestioning. Ulfilas was not their favourite writer. They didn't think he was a good read any more than I did. He'd given them a nasty surprise, too. But they sighed and got down to it, arriving in class with their tidy files and flawless handwriting. If you had to do Gothic to get a degree in English, so be it. They were not ones for teach-ins, sit-ins, picket lines, boycotts and protests. That came much later. Most of them were very up-front Christians and that turned out to be important for me. The bits of Gothic we had to translate were from the New Testament. I recollect that one was that passage about 'where moth doth corrupt and thieves break in and steal'. Another was the Lord's Prayer.

I had never read the New Testament. The very idea of reading it was distasteful to me. This was not a religious objection. I wasn't religious. I didn't go to synagogue except to keep my grandfather company on the few occasions when he went as an act of solidarity. My scant, rote-learnt Hebrew was disappearing fast. No, getting into the New Testament would be like going over to the other side, kissing its icons. The name Jesus I found difficult to say. He was their Man, not mine. My Christian classmates, of course, were not finding translation the least bit difficult, if you can call it translation. They scarcely had to look at the Gothic — they knew that stuff by heart. I ask you, the Lord's Prayer! At eighteen I might have heard of it but I certainly didn't know it.

Gif uns himma daga....

Give us this day....

Perhaps Dr Brookfield knew why I was having difficulty, or partly knew. If she did she gave not the slightest indication. But then, none of the lecturers ever gave a flicker of awareness that *The Jew of Malta* or *The Merchant of Venice* or *The Prioresse's Tale* might be making me resentfully uncomfortable. We were doing literature, not politics. And, as someone once said, maybe English is not a university subject for Jews.

So it was that I seethed in the first few classes and spent far too many hours preparing bloody Ulfilas while the young women could spare time mugging up Germanic sound changes, the Great Vowel Shift, Grimm's Law, Verner's Law. One of them said to me one day

"You're a funny chap, Rosen, you really are. All you've got to do is buy yourself a copy of the New Testament." And then she added wickedly, "Still, you might lose a grievance that way."

She was right. I had to get a New Testament. If translating bits of it was a kind of betrayal, imagine what a total defection buying it would be, actually walking into a shop

70

and buying one. This was to give a home to their Book on my shelves. To hear coming out of it their words. Buy it I couldn't. Remember, no one had ever said to me that I mustn't read that book. I don't think they ever referred to it. They banned it by silence. Yet I knew how shocked they would be if they knew that my course obliged me to buy it and read it. I exaggerate, there were some people at home who would not have turned a hair and maybe even laughed. My Uncle Sam might have said, 'Comparative Religion, eh? Very advanced!'

I could go so far and no further. I was not going to buy it. Borrow one from the library maybe? Copy out chunks before returning it? Tedious. Suddenly the solution came to me and I laughed to myself at the beauty of the irony. The Mission to the Jews.

Philpot Street Synagogue was a large building disguised as a Greek temple with its fat columns and pediment. A few buildings further along the road was the Mission to the Jews. When I was young this seemed to me like a most wilful act of provocation but when I was a teenager a couple of friends and I found the Mission very funny and also enigmatic. We could not imagine any adult we knew ever going into the place. What for? What would they say? 'Good morning, I'd like to be a Christian. How long does it take, please? Does it cost?' Manny said,

"You ever heard of a Jew becoming a Christian? You couldn't make yourself into a *goy* even if you wanted to. You couldn't talk like one, you couldn't eat like one, you couldn't look like one."

"Henriques talks like one and looks like one."

"Oh, him. He's Sephardic, that's different. Even so, he hasn't become a Christian. He takes Jewish prayers in that boys' club of his."

"So you tell me. That building over there. Must cost a fortune. They do it all for nothing?"

We were sitting on a low wall opposite the mission. It was about five o'clock and we'd decided to settle a problem. We'd never seen anyone going in or out, would-be

71

convert or missionary. Who were they, these missionaries? What did they look like? How many were there? We soon found out. At their closing time, four of them came out of the front door, three men and a woman. They all wore sober clothes which we thought of as gentile and seemed to us, though I think we invented it, downcast and furtive. They certainly weren't sprightly in their step nor did they look round with good cheer. Manny said,

"And that lot think they're going to make us all Christians? Some hopes."

"Nice job, though, being a Jew-converter. You don't lift a finger, year in, year out, and get paid for it."

"You know, there's a woman in Varden Street married into a Jewish family. A *shiksa* she is — well, was — but she converted. Learnt all the prayers and everything. And what about Rutman's presser? Speaks Yiddish better than me and he's a *goy*. Old Rutman thinks it's marvellous. He keeps saying to him for a joke, 'Henry, you speak Yiddish so good you should get circumcised'."

"That's all different," said Manny. "There's no Mission to the Christians, is there? And there'd be a right *shemozzle* if there was. It's different, isn't it?" He didn't sound all that sure.

And now, just because of Ulfilas I was on my way to this same Mission to the Jews. The beauty of it was that I wasn't swallowing my pride and giving in to the quiet tyranny of old Ulfilas. I was going to put one over him. I pushed open the door and there in the large hall was a desk, all very neat. There were small stacks of pamphlets and a letter rack. Around the hall were posters with quotable bits of the New Testament in large black letters. And there were some in Hebrew. I hadn't expected that. I had expected lots of pictures of Jesus Christ extending his arms over little children with blond curls. Or the Crucifix. Of them not a sign. A man behind the desk looked up when I came in. I told myself that he was amazed. I had prepared my great *chutzpah* performance.

"Do sit down. Can I help?"

"Yes," I said firmly. "I have never read the New Testament, you see, and I'd very much like to do so." The man brightened up.

"Do you think I could borrow one for a short while?"

"Borrow one? We'd be happy to give you one."

He pulled open a drawer and with a touch of ceremony handed me a New Testament. I have it to this day. Soft black leather covers extending beyond the body of the book and fine rice paper made it flexible and different. I got up to go. But he wasn't going to let this occasion slip by so easily.

"Would you mind waiting just a moment? I'd like you to meet our Director."

He edged me into a nearby room. I hadn't bargained for this. The Director, a man with a gold watch chain across a black waistcoat, in no time was asking me questions. 'Was I a student? Why did I want to read the New Testament? Would I like to know more about Christianity? Would I like to meet a group of Christian students?' I improvised feebly, almost always with a lie. When they asked for my name and address ('to keep in touch') I invented them. They pressed pamphlets on me. I fled from the place, knowing things hadn't turned out to be such a laugh after all. But I had my New Testament and when I next saw Manny I gave him a full report.

"I missed being baptised by a whisker."

I was still sufficiently aggrieved about the Ulfilas business to be determined to be quite open with my New Testament. I went into class, smiled at the others and spread it out at the right page. When my turn came I consulted it with slow deliberation. Dr Brookfield drew up alongside me.

"Mr Rosen," she said as quietly as ever, "have you prepared this passage?

"Most carefully, Dr Brookfield."

"In that case, why do you need this crib?"

She lifted the New Testament, rather irreverently, I thought. By now I was sick of the childishness of it all.

"No, Dr Brookfield, this is not a crib, as you call it. This is your New Testament."

She was taken aback and I instantly regretted my improvised rudeness and wished I could withdraw it.

"Well," she said, "in this class my New Testament is, I am afraid, a crib and using it is not fair to the others."

"No," I said, "can't you see that the whole of this class is unfair to me?"

I closed my books, stood up, stumbled along the row and left the room.

Not Yet

Detention. Just six of us; the usual crimes, the usual criminals — me, Solly, Berko, Saxy, Mo (of course) and the unknown quantity, Hoffman. The crime sheet was so routine you could have run it off for the whole term on the old Gestetner. Talking in class, calling out, passing notes, homework not in on time, lying — conduct prejudicial to good order and discipline. All down in Brock's flawless hand. So flawless, so durable and ineradicable, it turned our follies and foibles into everlasting wickedness so that we despaired of ever going straight. But Hoffman was new, only two months with us, His clothes were more expensive than ours, dapper men's, not youth's, shoes and silk shirts. He was more pink than us, his hair was straight and fine and sandy. He was more suave too. We thought him, I hesitate, almost — well, Gentile. He was in for cheek rather than *chutzpah*. To Gobby with whom we had long since learned not to trifle. Gobby had been pursuing an earnest enquiry about nouns in apposition and drawn Hoffman into the quest. 'I've never been taught that — er, Sir.' Harmless enough, but this Hoffman could languidly imply that, if he hadn't been taught such things, they weren't worth knowing or at any rate he shouldn't be pestered about them. Gobby did his eye-flicker for a second or so and then struck, as we knew he would. He was suddenly affable even solicitous. — Ah yes. It has crossed my mind that your last school left you a little-er-unfinished. We can help a little. May I suggest you present yourself in Room 23 at 4 o'clock? Hoffman tried to get out a word...

"No need to thank me. You'll find it all works out best if you arrive strictly on time. Now take this example, 'Albert, the Prince Regent...'" And we were back on course. Meanwhile Hoffman had smiled gratefully at the unlooked for chance to study the detention system.

75

So here he was with the old lags looking less cast down and aggrieved than us and less tousled by the wear and tear of a school day. No ink on his hands. Tie and collar fit for a studio photograph, no marks of brawling or chesting a wet football. We mooched to the empty desks, sullen and grumpy but resigned, dumped ourselves down and dropped our satchels on the floor. We spread ourselves around like strangers, knowing if we didn't we'd only be separated in a minute or two. Hoffman hadn't moved yet. He slowly gave the whole room the once over, his inspection drifting past us. He made his fastidious choice and sauntered over to the desk nearest to the door under the baize notice-board, next to the fire-extinguisher. We watched him and his almost adult ways. Not our kind of adults though. Ours overfilled their clothes and spilled *schmalz* on them, they walked with their feet close to the ground, toes outwards, heads bent forward and turned towards each other, and they poked fingers into each other's shoulders. They were cocooned in communal noise, did not know about Private Persons. They all talked at once, shouted as they slapped down their dominoes at the Workers' Circle or slurped their lemon tea or bitterly cursed the tailoring trade in noisy knots at the corner of Great Garden Street. No, what the adult Hoffman was shaping up for was more like those occasional figures you saw stalking down the Whitechapel Road who came from Outside and made your mind shuffle uneasily at the faint whiff of power they gave off. They dealt with others, haunted offices or inspected something and never looked to right or left to catch sight of a relative or someone from the same *shtetl* back in the East. Up there in the Sixth Form where they put on white coats to do Zoology there were one or two who were beginning to get the knack and might soon pass themselves off as the real thing. Golly Gottlieb came to school with a rolled umbrella and he was going to study at the London School of Economics, whatever that was. Gluckstein, whose father owned the big furniture shop opposite the Jewish Reading Room, had taken to wearing a fine light grey suit which clearly had not come out of the tailoring dens off the Commercial Road. A lawyer he was going to be and he had already closed his face to get into that part. Had they stopped eating pickled herring and *latkes*? Maybe you could learn how to do it. But then they couldn't have been the sort who had landed up regularly in detention when they were in the third year. Hoffman's kind of adult we saw in the pictures at the Rivoli or Palaseum, poised possessors of occasions, velvet public movers, who knew how to stand, walk or confer the benefit of themselves on a chair, always affable but always inviolable. But this Hoffman wasn't out of a film and was no Sixth Former. New he might be, but his lot was cast in with ours, a Third Former with an essay to do on *Henry IV Part One*, trying to get the hang of simultaneous equations, chanting defective Latin verbs for next Friday's test, listening to forty minutes uninterrupted droning on the Factory Acts and scribbling the notes from the board. What's more we'd noticed he wasn't too good at that kind of thing. As if that mattered. For the moment we were not competing furtively for B pluses and As but studying his glide over to the desk by the fire extinguisher and his so English manner of gracing the seat. It was already said by the know-all *yuchners* that he'd never been to *cheder* classes and, though this was beyond belief, that he'd not been *barmitzvah-ed*. Was that how you did it and got to be a Sixth Former before your time?

So we sat and endured the minutes. Mo was gently rattling coins in his pockets, Solly was drawing on the little pad he carried around, Saxy was whistling pianissimo through his teeth and drawn back lips, Berko cheated of his football was torturing himself by listening to the sound of the ball being thumped about outside. I was looking at Hoffman. He was leaning back in his seat and waiting, it seemed from the beginnings of a rosy smile, for a performance to begin.

If anything stirred beneath our torpor it was speculation about who would be the master in charge of this detention.

And it mattered. If it was going to be Burroughs, he would give out dictionaries, select an arbitrary page and you copied out entries for an hour. 'Wouldn't want to be wasting your precious time,' he would say. Leggy would make us sit in total silence, arms folded, eyes front. (All of them had been in the army). Then he'd read his paper or savagely mark books. He once crossed out a page of my futile maths with such ferocity that his red pencil slashed the page open. He had to be watched, for he had a filthy temper and we had just enough prudence to be wary of him. In detentions he would glance up often enough to take a good *shufti* at us and spot a backslider who would be made to stand facing the wall with his nose touching it. O'Shea on the other hand made it clear that he was bored out of his mind himself and he just used to chat with us and encourage us to be ever so slightly cheeky.

"Where d'you buy suits like that?" We'd ask about his rural peatbrown Harris tweed the like of which we'd never clapped eyes on.

"Buy 'em? You don't buy 'em. They get handed down as heirlooms."

"Did you really play hockey for your university?"

"Yes," he'd say, "we didn't win a ghost of a match that year. And don't be prying so much."

"Which football team do you support?"

"And why should I be supporting a football team? Haven't I got my work cut out supporting meself and me aged mother? I won't be taking on a football team till I'm a Headmaster and mebbe even then, the money won't run to it."

We had just begun to detect the Celtic fringe amongst our teachers and had a dim and wildly inaccurate notion of what it all amounted to. But a kind of humour came into it somewhere and anyway O'Shea was good value, especially in the deserts of detentions. Imagine trying to talk to Gobby like that. No, that would be like trying to imagine him with his trousers down or doing a Highland fling. When Gobby took detention you stayed on the alert every second. No Yiddish obscenities and curses meant to be just heard but not understood, no deaf-and-dumb signals across the spaces, no scamping of chores, no ostentatious shufflings and coughings, no slumping from mock exhaustion as the clock dragged towards five, no cross-legged squirmings and asking to be excused and staying for five minutes to watch the football. No nothings with Gobby. You could forget the whole repertoire of diversions from tedium and illicit resistances. Gobby never raised his voice, never gave a sign of teacherly outrage or distress, just that sinister flicker of the eyelids, a slight pursing of the lips, a sniff or two, the handkerchief drawn from the sleeve, dab, dab, then a stiletto sentence. With him it was all heads down and not a whimper of rebellion.

It turned out in a minute or two that it was Mr King's stint for the detention shift. We called him Queenie not just to turn the world verbally upside down nor even because we saw him as a homosexual. We knew neither the word nor the idea. It was just that he moved, talked and engaged with us in ways we knew only from women. Even his public school speech was the soft caressing variety you hear in some artists and writers — all the same sounds but articulated in a different place and with a different music coaxed out of them. Poor old Queenie! He might just as well have presented his jugular to ravening wolves as come amongst us with his alien kind of chivalry, gentleness and vulnerability, his inability to disguise his hurt at rejection and mockery. Easy enough to recognise years later that there was a man it would have been good to know and learn from, but then he was nothing more than a perfect prey, a *goy* with a difference. He belonged to that little band of folk who are not made for this wicked world, should not be let out alone. They must be protected, taken round ambushes, have their tickets bought for them and be put on trains while they are freed to go on thinking about Baudelaire. He was certainly no person to send into the lair of Yiddisher *knuckers*, coarse clever-dicks ever on the look-out for a rare sacrificial victim. We'd never run into his like, someone both clever and easily wounded, articulate but without a repertoire of put-downs, humiliated but not a humiliator, knowledgeable about books but not about boys. Poor fellow, he paid for it all. We sacrificed him without remorse. Such a *schmeryl*! Strange revenges for our own hurts which we could not have put in words flowed against him. Without personal animosity we demolished him and scored it up as a little victory, against all the nameless defeats. What a misfortune to be a nice man without a shell amongst such frustrated predators.

Queenie came bouncing into the room with all the simulated energy of the fearful. Insubordination flickered into life immediately and Queenie was saying through the escalating disorder. 'Now, look chaps. Do something sensible, eh. You can start on your homework. It'll save you time later. Read a book. The hour will go more quickly. Or why don't you...' We orchestrated a huge clatter with our satchels, complained about empty ink-wells, chuntered to each other mimicking and mocking his speech, turning it into foppish silliness. We half-began a bit of reading or set about an exercise. Queenie teetered on the edge of total impotence and we teetered on the edge of open defiance and worse. I do not like to think about it now. It's not only a squeamish recoil from the cruelties. Nor is it that a mere eight years later I was on the receiving end, having gone over to the enemy. It is because I know now why we were pitted against one another in the detention room and that poor Queenie could never have known where it had all gone wrong for him. He had his first class French degree (Cantab.) and a gown. Why had he been set down amongst these pitiless torturers, with their outlandish names and outlandish noises?

We were all in it except Hoffman. He was eye-ing Queenie in his long black gown, and was leaning back in his seat, not joining in with the rest of us, just steadily watching the fluttering and flappings of the wounded bird — in a nicely restrained sort of way, a well-balanced spectator in the better part of the house.

We simmered and simmered towards five o'clock. If it had been the whole class, we would have erupted but a scattered handful we kept an eye on the boundaries. Solly's thumb and forefinger had a frozen hold on the top of a page of a textbook. Berko had written a few scratchy lines in an exercise book. If Queenie's glance lighted on him, he advertised himself as someone grappling with difficult ideas. In between foghorn yawns Saxy was fiddling with his maths homework. He loved the damn stuff really. And Mo was keeping up a grumbling mutter, looking up occasionally to the ceiling with his eyes shut and then down to an open book: this was his regular learning-something-by-heart performance. Oh yes. We each had our little fail-safe system on the go. We didn't overdo it. The work was at best sporadic but just enough. Between whiles there was a good laugh. Berko could belch at will and control the volume and texture to suit the occasion or his fancy. He chose his moments to crackle and rumble knowing his virtuosity and variety always had us in fits.

"Ach, such a filthy *chuzza!*" We applauded.

The rule book laid down the iron laws of a well-run detention but some teachers worked their own little variations. If you were in luck, at about half-time, they'd leave you to it and nip up to the staff room. A teacher would look round at the class, assure himself we were moderately cowed, walk up and down the rows a couple of times to uncover any illicit goings-on. (A comic, I remember, was a very illicit going-on or any kind of sweet-popping.) Then he'd make slowly for the door and turn for a last quelling stare. We'd glisten with good behaviour and pray. And he'd be gone. A calculated brief silence just in case. And then...

"All right for him. I'm busting for a piss."

"Gone for a quick drag."

"A quick drag! With that pipe. It'll take him till five to get it going."

"Doing his betting slips."

"Chaim Schmerl went to the races.

Lost his *gutgas* and his braces..."

"Such a voice! A *chazan* we should make of him."

Then we'd shush each other up and drop to whispers while the detention master took his ease in the Staff Room. None of us had ever been into that secret lair. At most you got a glimpse of billowing tobacco smoke, dusty tomes, tatty old leather armchairs, huge heaps of grimy exercise books and a flickering coal fire. Where else in the world could there be a room like it? Gobby once sent me up to get Funk and Wagnell's Dictionary on a dull winter's evening. The gaunt joyless Brock stood in the doorway without his gown, the keeper of Hell's Gate. Behind him I caught a glimpse of the other masters floating eerily in the smoke touched by the light of the fire. They seemed dead and doomed.

No point in Queenie waiting for a lull. He took his chance, left us to our bogus work and bolted out of the door.

Hoffman said, it's 4.27, and crossed off another minute in his Rough Work Book. Then he swung his legs out from under the desk and stretched them out over the top. There were sharp creases in his trousers. Berko moved to the window to watch the footballers who were doing without him. Someone behind me was patiently picking a hole in the thick oak desk top with his geometry compass. Suddenly Hoffman said in a loud voice, how does this thing work? He was lightly tapping the fire-extinguisher above his head. It didn't sound like a serious question All the same we all turned towards him. Berko turned his head from the window and the woodpecker behind me stopped tap-tapping.

"Tells you on the side."

The fire-extinguisher we all knew. Amongst all the battered wood, splintered parquet, scratched brown varnish, pock-marked tiles and flaking distemper its gorgeous red, black and gold looked like a mistake. In every classroom they were untouched and untouchable. We'd all read the instructions 'In case of fire...' and so forth. Please God, we'd never need to use it. Enough trouble without emergencies. Emergency exits; in emergency use hammer to break windows; the coiled hose; life-belts; high voltage; electrified rails, do not cross the lines. Emergencies we could do without.

"Don't you know then?" said Hoffman.

Mo couldn't resist.

"There's a sort of hammer fixed to the side. And there's that pin. Stops you moving the hammer. When you pull the pin out, you can move the hammer up and down. You just lift the hammer up and bash it down on the side and that..." Mo stopped as he realised Hoffman was listening seriously and taking note.

But Hoffman said, "That sounds really stupid. Don't believe a word of it, Pins and hammers. You don't expect me to swallow that, do you?"

"He's *meshiggah*," Solly whispered to me. We were uneasy. We had our sense of things getting out of hand.

Hoffman was on his feet. A panicky voice said, Leave it, Hoffman. But Hoffman already had the pin out and was looking contemptuously at us. He lifted the hammer and let it drop onto the side of the extinguisher. Clonk! Nothing happened.

"You see?" said Hoffman, "you're so stupid. It doesn't work like that."

We were getting desperate. Little wickednesses were one thing but sin on this scale was beyond us. There would be some terrible retribution. Grand audacity was for others.

"You're right, you're right," we told him. "Only leave the bloody thing alone. You'll damage it. Just leave it alone, leave it alone."

Hoffman fingered the hammer again. We were squeaking with cowardly anxiety.

"We'll all cop it. God knows what they'll do to us."

Hoffman found our performance distasteful. Swiftly he turned his back on us, lifted the hammer and smashed it down against the fire extinguisher. White foam came gushing out of the nozzle and hit the front of the class-room, a gorgeous white froth, unstoppable and wondrous. We fell into a bewitched silence. Hoffman grabbed the thing from the wall and sprayed it nonchantly about, having the time of his life.

"Should be put away, the *schmendrik*. Certified —"

"Locked-up."

We palpitated with shock and delight. The foam began to spread over the floor, over the desks and around our feet. It was irresistible. We started kicking it about, romping in it, shouting with abandon. White flecks spattered on trousers and jackets.

"Get it out of here! Shove it in the corridor! Stick it in the book cupboard!

We hoped he wouldn't. Hoffman's posture had become heroic. He pointed the nozzle like a fixed bayonet. He would hold out till the last round. There should have been a camera.

The foam still gushed. Somewhere beyond our jolly paddling and splashing a nerve of panic still throbbed.

"Get Queenie," Saxy said. We laughed our heads off at such a delicious possibility. Queenie in this madhouse. Saxy wasn't joking. He paddled out of the room and was back in no time with a flushed Queenie struggling to look masterful and cool. He was on the edge of tears. He rushed madly at Hero Hoffman to grab the extinguisher. Hoffman somehow didn't time his release too well. By the time Queenie was in full-possession after the badly-managed transfer there were gobbets of foam down the front of Queenie's suit. He steadied himself and adjusted his grip while the extinguisher sprayed around wildly. We faked terror, ducking and side-stepping.

Queenie shouted, "Open a window, open a window. That one."

Two of us wrestled for the window pole. The winner waved it around the catch, found it and tugged. We egged him on, choking on our laughter. And while the foam still sprayed Queenie hopped up and down with the fire extinguisher as though he were holding a bomb. He wanted none of it, having no taste for emergencies himself. His face was bright red and creased with anxiety.

At last the window squeaked open and Queenie rushed up to it. With his only touch of masterly control he directed the nozzle out of the window. At his first go the jet hit a window pane but he adjusted his aim and got on target. The creases dropped from his face. But at the very moment of his triumph the stream of foam curled into a weak arc. Queenie stood his ground as though hoping for better things. And then a last feeble dribble splashed onto the floor. Queenie's shoulders dropped and he let the extinguisher hang from his hands.

To a man we burst into cheers and jumped up and down beside ourselves. All caution gone we let rip, mounting a huge din.

"You silly, silly man," I heard Hoffman saying while clapping appreciatively.

Suddenly, Queenie turned on us hugging the gleaming red extinguisher, his legs apart. Yes, I was sure now, his eyes were brimming with tears. The cheers died slowly into a silence. Queenie came a step nearer. Out of his anguish he yelled.

"What do you people come here for? What do you want of us?"

As if we knew. Perhaps Hoffman did. But we didn't. Not for sure. Not yet.

Penmanship

All Mr O'Carroll's teaching of writing skills rested on the one foundation principle — 'Up thin, down thick'. He was a methodical man and as a writing master his procedure was unvarying. He walked up and down the rows, cane in hand to achieve a classful of impeccable calligraphers who no longer made aitches without loops, zeds and kays without their twiddly bits or mutated their Qs into gees. He walked up and down the rows, cane in hand and if you malformed a letter you put out your hand and got a stinger, delivered without mercy or malice. Up and down he went, swishing away for half an hour. This reign of terror may have worked well for some but it made my pen falter and the faint chance I had of turning out a page without blots and exotic shapes for letters vanished in my despair and resignation. Resigned I certainly was. On the day when I could see that my kay, the old enemy, had gone astray again, Mr O'Carroll was right over the other side of the room dispassionately dispensing just deserts. I realised I'd have a long wait before he got round to me. I put up my hand.

"Please, sir, my kay, I've done my kay wrong. Can I have the cane now?"

Mr O'Carroll obliged and, crossing the room, delivered a whack and coolly went back to where he had left off. Give him his due, he always caned the left hand. So I tucked my hand under my arm and took up again the deformed writer's crouch. I'm afraid Mr O'Carroll put the final touches on the making of an illegible handwriter and was the cause later on of all those infuriated teachers' cries of 'I'm not even going to try to read this scribble' and 'Fit for the waste-paper basket' and those sneery remarks at the bottom of my written work in the grammar school. 'This may be the work of a genius but no one will ever know.' I couldn't very well explain to them that it was all Mr

O'Carroll's fault and about that cane doing overtime and up-thin-and-down-thick.

I had one last chance to reform and, who knows, to produce manuscripts I could feel good about instead of being embarrassed by their sheer ugliness. Much of my disgruntlement was due to the fact that my scrawl was exposed day after day to my teachers' grimaces. My classmates would take a peek, too.

"Didn't know you could write Yiddish."

"A doctor, that's what you're going to be. You've got the writing for it."

"It's a code, a secret code."

I had this last chance, as I said, when I started in the grammar school. I knew we were going to do prestigious and snobby things like French, Latin and Physics, and go to a proper sports field and have a cap badge with a galleon and French motto on it, *Tel grain, Tel pain*. We were the elect, swept up into a rarefied air, laced with the scent of privilege. Then came a terrible blow that brought us down to earth. They told us we would be having a handwriting class. We were incredulous, insulted, humiliated. Kids' stuff. The ones whose penmanship was already as good as any adult's and whose hands raced and looped lightly across the page were sure it couldn't mean what it said. It was bound to be some kind of special writing.

"Special writing," someone said, "like you see on parchment. You do it with a feather pen. Lawyers have to do it."

"It's like the way they write the *Torah* scrolls. You have to do it perfect. You have to do it perfect."

"That's more what you call lettering, not handwriting. They said handwriting, not lettering."

Though I joined in the outrage at being demoted in this way I secretly thought that there was just a chance that I might redeem myself and learn to write decently. So I hoped they were wrong about lettering, parchment and all that. They should be so lucky.

When the time came we were all taken by surprise, The teacher gave out something he called copybooks. We had never seen such things before. In fact even at that time most people would have regarded them as museum pieces. They looked like ordinary exercise books but they had 'Copybooks' printed on the cover and when you opened them you discovered that on each page there were printed in faultless copperplate four or five sentences like Procrastination is the thief of Time, Cleanliness is next to Godliness, The child is father to the man, Necessity is the mother of invention. Underneath each of these improving sentiments there were three lines, just like on our millboards in Miss Campbell's class when we were babies. We were expected to produce perfect replicas of the copperplate models. The class set to work, fizzing with resentment.

"If my poppa saw me doing this he'd have a fit," said Barney. "He thinks we spend all day showing how clever we are like *yeshiva bochers*."

"Not my dad. Know what he'd say? 'So what's wrong with learning to write nice? Those people know what they're doing, I'm telling you. A degree every one of them's got. Nothing wrong with learning to write like a *mensch*.'"

I don't know how a *mensch* writes but it was soon clear to me that even with the severe guidance of the model lines of copperplate my writing wasn't going to get any better. When we finally parted with the copybooks at the end of the term, everyone, myself included, reverted to the style they'd been using for years. No one's looked like copperplate. Not one of our teachers had handwriting that was faintly like copperplate. They made no comment about all this and the copybook exercise was treated as a ritual, the origin of which had been forgotten but which was kept up for good form's sake.

Between the First Year and the Fifth Year my writing got worse and worse, partly because we spent so many hours scribbling notes from the board and partly because I was always rushing my homework in the hope of leaving time to join the boys in the street. Mr Gunn, the History teacher, wrote quite beautifully on the board and very fast, too. If you didn't keep up with him he was wiping it off and starting on the next bit. Lazy Mr Powell sat on his desk, swinging his legs, fingering his little moustache and dictating at a speed nobody could keep up with. Too fast, too fast, some of us would shout. It made no difference. He swept on, caring no more about our protests than he cared about the geography he was supposed to be teaching. We prayed for a break when he would draw a map on the board, a diagrammatic one on which we could not distinguish between land and sea, rivers and boundaries. I decided in the end that the reason he'd taken to dictation was that his writing, too, was quite illegible. I had seen a page in the notebook he was dictating from when I went to the front to use the pencil sharpener. That didn't stop him crossing out my homework and writing, 'Hasty, sloppy and unreadable. Re-write. See me.' I saw him alright, at the end of the day. He'd obviously forgotten what it was all about.

"My work," I said. "The Amazon. You said I've got to re-write it."

"Got it with you? No? I might have guessed. I remember now. Well, I'm not having it, my boy. Do you really expect me to spend hours and hours trying to read your stuff?"

"No, sir."

"Well, I can tell you this much. Anything you write in the exam which looks like your usual mess will not be marked. You'll get nought. Get this into your noddle. The examiners are told that they're not obliged to read your kind of writing. You'll get nought. The thing is that your writing — I mean it's so uneducated — not a peasant, are you?"

So he got The Amazon 'in best' as we used to say. Usually anything Mr Powell said didn't leave a lasting impression on me but we were getting very close to the matric exams. In addition to the anxieties we all shared — do I know enough to pass? — I was now alarmed at the possibility that the examiners would not even read my work.

Our teachers often invoked the examiners who gradually grew in our thoughts to become implacable, omniscient ogres who wouldn't give a second thought to brushing pages of desperate work into the waste paper basket. They would settle my hash at a glance. I was very rattled. The shadows of the ever-punitive examiners darkened my frenetic revision. Abe, who was revising with me in the evenings, lost his patience.

"Why do you let a *pisher* like Powell put the wind up you? *Er veist nisht fon der hant un der fis*. He doesn't know his arse from his elbow. Did you ever get nought for the end of year exams? For the mock exams? So leave off grizzling, will you?"

I remained inconsolable.

It takes some believing but only a month or two earlier my writing had been in demand. I wrote loveletters for a sailor. I was in the Reading Room of the Whitechapel Library where some of us used to do our homework. A wiry little chap slid into the seat next to me and started muttering something or other. Eventually it turned out that he was a sailor whose ship had docked somewhere in the Thames nearby and that he needed to write to his beloved in Liverpool. He pushed a cheap little writing pad under my nose and asked me to do the job for him. It was obvious to me that he couldn't write but at first I assumed he'd dictate in whispers and I would simply be his scribe. (Me, his scribe!) But no, he wanted me to compose as well and it had to be a loveletter. Somehow he made all this clear. I don't remember what I wrote though I could make a good guess. I'd not yet written any loveletters myself but I had read a lot of novels and with shameless confidence I wrote a nice devoted piece to Agnes in Liverpool. My sailor watched my writing flowing out of my pen as though I were performing magic. He couldn't take his eyes off it. I whispered my text back to him and did the envelope. He took the letter and envelope and pushed sixpence across to me — the first money I earned by my writing in both senses of the word. I did the same job for him half a dozen times and then my sailor stopped coming to the Reading Room which was just as well because he never showed me replies from Agnes, if there were any, and I was running out of ideas. At the time I was grimly amused by the fact that I was earning money from my penmanship while my teachers waged an unceasing and ineffectual war against it. I wonder how Agnes managed.

There were ten days to go until the exams. We were at our sports field for athletics trials. Winners would represent the school and I hoped to be one of them. I'd run the half mile and was now doing the long jump. I was not what you'd call a brilliant long jumper but probably the best the school could come up with for the under-sixteens. It was a lean year. Facilities in those days were primitive: the long jump pit was far too narrow and the run up was on worn wet grass. My third jump. I made an over-anxious flailing effort to do a hitch-kick which I'd read about in a book. I landed awkwardly and hit my elbow, my left elbow, on the brass rule at the side of the pit. During the rest of the afternoon it became very painful and swollen. The teacher in charge advised me to go to the hospital when I got back — to be on the safe side, as he said. I could get straight off the tram from the sports field and into the London Hospital on the Whitechapel Road. At the hospital a sporty young doctor listened to my story and asked me how far I'd jumped on that third jump and I had to admit that it was such a bad jump I hadn't stopped to find out.

"I long jump for the Hospital. Hard on the ankle and the Achilles. But the elbow, that's a new one. Let's get it X-rayed."

I wanted to ask him how you jumped for a hospital but didn't want to sound stupid. The upshot was that I had broken my elbow and went home with my arm in a sling and feeling shaky. My mother took one look at the sling and, for once forgetting to drown me in sympathy, clapped her hand to her face and said,

"Your exams! How are you going to do them? *Gottinue*! Were you out of your mind? Fooling around just before your exams! What were you thinking of? What did they say to you at the hospital? Broken! *Vey iz meine yahren*, broken! Such a fine time to do long jumping. You couldn't wait till after exams, so urgent it was. You're not studying long jumping. You don't do matric in long jumping."

She sat down and rocked to and fro as though there'd been a death in the family.

"Mum, it's my left arm. The doctor showed me the X-ray. It's just a little crack. Anyone would think it had been amputated."

"God forbid. Don't even say such things. Such jokes he makes."

The next morning my form master at registration was full of concern and wanted to know the whole story. As the exams grew near most of our teachers underwent a change of heart. Slowly they changed sides and joined us as confederates in efforts to outwit the implacable examiners. By subtle analysis of past papers they tried to forecast questions and suggested ingratiating little turns of phrase we might use. My form master was not quite as frantic as my mother but shared her anxiety.

"Your writing, Rosen. It's not a work of art at the best of times but with that arm..."

"It's my left arm, sir."

"Yes, but you have to rest on it and that sling will throw you out of balance."

He spoke as though he was trying to convince himself and me, rehearsing something.

"Leave this to me. I'll write to the University."

Write to the University! To me that was like writing to God. What would he say? A few days later he beckoned to me. I went to the front of the room and he took out of an envelope a little wodge of papers.

"Read it," he said. "It'll cheer you up."

I took the top sheet. It looked like a diploma with the University of London's crest at the top. It read:

This candidate 05774 has recently broken his arm. This has adversely affected his handwriting and examiners are

93

required to take this into account when marking his papers.

My heart sang. I'd tried out my writing by then and it was the same old ugly scrawl. My arm in a sling had not made a scrap of difference. But They wouldn't know.

"There'll be one of those pinned to every paper," said my form-master. "Should help a bit."

Believe it or not, he winked, that old comrades-in-crime gesture from one of my teachers! Abe wanted to know all about it.

"Recently broken his arm," I quoted. "And it didn't say which one."

"That's one thing you can stop moaning about then," said Abe. "Arm in a sling, everyone should have one. Mind you, that's what I call perfect timing."

I was so ecstatic that I felt as though I had already passed my exams. Even the examiners' iron hearts would melt when they read those notices. I could hear them saying,

"Tough on the lad. And he's churned out a readable script."

I imagined them giving me the benefit of several doubts, nudging me across a border or two and enjoying the feel of magnanimity in doing so. In each exam a slip from the University was placed on my desk and when things weren't going too well the sight of it consoled me. How could they fail a boy with a broken arm?

I passed. I got my Matric and went on to the Sixth Form. Well, you never know. Those beautiful slips may have just seen me through. Without them I might, like many of my friends, have ended up as a clerk in the City — if my writing had been good enough.

Millions of hand-written words later my writing doesn't seem to baffle anybody. In the Sixth Form I taught myself to write very small and not to swoop erratically across the page but lightly to push the pen up and down. It gradually became a sensual pleasure. It feels nice and I enjoy seeing a page of text unwinding from my pen. The word processor, calling for eight fidgety fingers, cheats me of the pleasures it took so long to develop. My thoughts don't go tap-tap. They inscribe themselves in an idiosyncratic flow. So against all the odds I end up with Roland Barthes and celebrate the 'joyous physical experience' of the calligrapher.

Missing Person

Hamlet:	My father, methinks I see my father.
Horatio:	0 where, my lord?
Hamlet:	In my mind's eye, Horatio.

Where's your father? they used to ask me. I choked on the
answer because it wasn't the name of a place and because
it was a story which in my early childhood I couldn't bear
to tell, a story I yearned to untell or transmute into ordinariness. Where's your father? concerned old *boobas* asked
me in neighbours' houses and I was ashamed to have to
say he wasn't where all other fathers were, where all my
friends' fathers were, at their mothers' sides. *Ay, ay*, the
boobas would say, and look down to their laps. Where's
your father? asked Mr Kelk in the Elementary School
when I'd written a composition about my family. I picked
up my pen and wrote another sentence for him, 'My father
is in America' and I spelled America wrongly and hung my
head.

As far as I can tell all people without a father in the
home, either because he's dead or in one way or another
totally absent, know just how his ghost and the myths
which cling to it stalk through their dreams, waking and
sleeping, how their childhood lives are inhabited by this
palpable absence. Where's your father? asks Jane Miller.
She's a good friend and she says the refusal of my father
to appear in the stories requires some sort of explanation.
I admit you could be baffled. But that's no bad thing.
Readers should be baffled. But you could also be intolera-
bly frustrated, another matter entirely. Well, I'll set the
records straight and, while I am about it, settle one or two
other matters. Whether it makes any difference to how
you read the stories, I can't tell.

When I was three years of age, my mother, after ten or
more years in America, decided to come home to her fam-

ily in the East End of London. We crossed New York where I thought the skyscrapers were going to fall on our taxi and was consoled by chunks of cake from a black leather bag. We boarded the USS President Harding. With us were also my older sister aged five and my younger brother, a toddler of two years. There's a photo of the four of us at the foot of a companionway. My mother looks strained and the three of us clinging to her skirts are frowning at the camera. A classic immigration picture in its way.

We had left behind my father, Morris, and two brothers, Laurie aged fifteen and Sidney, aged seventeen. The time came when my mother set about explaining why our father and brothers hadn't followed us. According to her, my father had been due to come as soon as he had scraped together the fares for the three of them. He never did and none of us in England ever saw him again. For a short while my father wrote regularly and sent some money. Then, some months after our arrival, my younger brother, Wally, died of pneumonia. It was the next part of my mother's story which stood out from the rest and which I replayed over and over again in my head. It was also the bit which I could never bear to tell when they asked, Where's your father? After my brother's death my father's letters changed from affectionate to violently recriminatory and he accused my mother of unforgivable neglect. Very soon, to her utter desolation, his letters and the money stopped, though for a while he wrote to my sister who had been a favourite and sent her a dollar or two. I was very jealous of those dollars. There was one bitter irony about my father's accusations. My mother had watched my brother die in hospital on November the eleventh, Armistice Day. She was making her way home blindly through the streets when she became aware of angry and threatening looks from the people around her. She had not heard the guns sounding for the Two Minutes Silence which meant so much in the years so close to the end of the First World War. Then it dawned on her what was happening. Only then did she begin to weep.

As we grew older we asked her why he had been so uncaring and cruel, why he had deserted us. She put it down to a wild and desperate grief at my brother's death. At other times she would claim it was beyond her understanding. We accepted her story for years and years yet anyone reading it now can see that it won't bear close scrutiny. I went on believing it well into adulthood when I eventually told myself that it didn't hang together very well. Why had she come to England without him in the first place? Was there another woman whom my mother had known about? Had there been a big final crisis quarrel? Had they been more incompatible than she had ever hinted? Her story surely must have been partly concocted to make it palatable to young children, to enable her to salvage some self-respect and she had repeated it often enough for it to become canonical. There was a hinterland I would never come to know. I never had the heart to tax her with my doubts.

Now you know why my father does not appear in my stories. In the early years of my childhood I constructed him as a handsome, powerful and loving man, a phantom who one day was certainly going to step from the shadows, reclaim us all and whisk us away to happiness. But conflicting ideas live together happily in the mind so long as an impermeable membrane keeps them apart. So I had no difficulty in believing at the same time that my mother had been tragically ill-used by him and agreed with the grown-ups at home, who saw him as a despicable wife-deserter. Then, too, there was the fact that both my brothers ran away from him, one to enlist in the American army and the other in the British army. No-one ever said why. It was always easier to keep the unblemished myth going because my mother never denounced my father. On the contrary, she fed my dreams with tales: how everyone admired his cleverness and quickness of tongue, how meticulous he was in his dress, what a fearless socialist

99

activist and trade unionist he was, standing in local elections and victimised out of his job for organising the union.

So there was my mother at something less than forty, only a year away from being installed in a home with a husband and five children, now a penniless single parent with her youngest dead and her two oldest turned into runaways. She had gone back to the small family house in the East End where she had grown up, ruled over by my stern matriarchal grandmother. Seven adults and a child were already somehow or another packed in.

My father remained over the years in deep freeze as a portrait photo which I still have, showing him, a good-looking young man in his twenties with a lot of black curly hair and a high white collar, a portrait annotated by what my mother had chosen to tell. Whereas when I was young he invaded my thoughts many, many times, especially when I felt hard done by (he would have shown them), gradually he faded away into a remote figure I could contemplate without anger, hurt or embarrassment. And there had certainly been times when it was not so, when they kept asking, Where's your father?

When I was twelve, for instance, my mother was finding it desperately difficult to cope with keeping me at the grammar school, for my scholarship grant didn't cover all the costs. Winter was coming and she knew she couldn't afford the expense of winter clothes for me. She swallowed her pride and her principles at one go and applied for help from those East End benefactors, the Jewish Board of Guardians, which was run by Jews who had made it, solid loyal citizens, many of whom came from old rich Sephardic families, well-rooted in the establishment. They even looked like *goyim* to me. They modelled themselves on respectable English institutions and what better precedents were there than *noblesse oblige* and the Poor Law. They met in a very official building at the end of Petticoat Lane, full of sombre wood, polished brass and smileless portraits of Jewish eminences with trim beards and expensive tiepins. We sat in a waiting room on big chairs and my mother coached me in whispers, took off my cap and tidied my hair with her hand. Eventually I was called in. Behind a long table covered in green baize, the Guardians were waiting for me, worthies with judicious faces and gold watchchains across their waistcoats. By what processes were they appointed to dole out obligatory food to the poor and to decide who did and who did not merit a handout?

About two yards in front of the table they had placed a chair. Sit down, Harold, someone was saying. I felt humiliated already, vulnerable, afraid of saying the wrong thing. Then came the grilling. Who lived at our house? How many were in work? What was the name of my school? What subjects was I studying? Did I get good marks? How much did my scholarship grant amount to? And so on. Then someone asked,

"Your father, my boy, what is his trade?"

I sweated and swallowed. I groped.

"He's... my father is... my father's job. He isn't here. I don't know his job."

"Well, where exactly is your father?"

The old unanswerable question. Before I could answer there was whispering back there and shuffling of dossiers.

"Never mind that now. Do you have to pay for your school textbooks?"

The Guardians deliberated and they gave my mother some vouchers for a suit and footwear. Money might so easily be misspent. The vouchers were only valid at one establishment in the Lane which turned out to be a kind of charity depot the Guardians had set up. Everything was on shelves in boxes and parcels. A sad little man took my measurements.

"The suit mebbe you won't like. We're not Cecil Gee's. But like iron it is. You can't wear it out if you try. And the boots, you wouldn't go to the Palais in them but for *lobbuses* in the school yard..."

He patted my back, consoling me. He was right. The suit was made of thick brown indestructible cloth and I only saw its like when I went with a team to play chess in the

Jewish Boys Orphanage in Norwood. All the boys wore suits just like that there. The heavy black boots I had to wear all that winter even though for us the boot age had long since passed.

I eventually composed a formula to deal with 'Where's your father?' Without batting an eyelid I would say, 'I haven't got a father.' This left them to decide whether I was an orphan or a bastard. I think they usually settled for orphan, more comfortable all round. Sometimes I brazenly said, he's dead, which cut out any further questions.

"Dead? *Uvver sholem*," they'd say, and leave it at that.

I see it all differently now, untinged, I hope, with self-pity. We were not an uniquely ill-fated family nor particularly unlucky. All over the world millions and millions of families and bits of families were and still are trekking across continents and oceans, harried by others and driven on by their fears and ambitions. How many wives lose their husbands, how many children their parents and each other? How many survivors would be glad to settle for one parent alive or a sister or brother? Besides, although something inescapably tragic clings about my memories of my mother's life — it is, after all, a sad story — she recovered rapidly from her disaster, as my stories show. It's true that she is sometimes a partly fictional figure in them but there's enough to show what a fighter she was. It was, after all, through her that I became a communist. She was the one above all who propelled me against the odds to go on to university education. Quite simply she believed in learning. When I was in the Sixth Form I read Frazer's *Golden Bough* and thought myself rarely intellectual. I took it home and she said, 'Fine book,' and began talking about it. Of course I was irritated. And here I am, what they call an Emeritus Professor and I still believe we need a better and quite different kind of society and I don't care whether you call it socialist or communist. I chafe inside the Labour Party, lamenting its timidities and mourning the days when there was a viable alternative. My mother said to me when she was old,

"I used to be sure that I'd see socialism here, in my day. Anyone can see that I won't. But you, you will live to see it in your day."

At my age that doesn't look likely and things don't look too promising for my sons. Perhaps I'll say the same as she did to my grandchildren sometime, but, if I do, it will be much more tentatively.

Everything I've worked for in education I can trace back to its beginnings in my family and its fierce radicalism and dogged hope which themselves grew out of an East End humming with politics. I don't want to explain everything in the stories which might give rise to questions. They must, like any stories, speak for themselves. In any case, I've not written an autobiography. I don't think I could — far too daunting. I have only rooted about in the depths of my past and grubbed up fragments which speak to me. It turned out they were all about my childhood and more particularly about my schooling. That must be because, rather late in the day, I revisited that distant world and interrogated it. That was when some of us were asking questions about the education of children from immigrant families who were settling into communities. What about their languages? What did it mean to be a member of a minority, to meet undisguised and dangerous hostility? I realised I'd been there already in my childhood. I used my scrutiny to help me understand bilingualism and what it means to be what Jane Miller calls a hybrid. When in the sixties and seventies it became fashionable to talk about the linguistic deprivation of the working class, I remembered the eloquence of the people amongst whom I grew up, not only those in the rag trade but also people like the dockers who sat in our living room and joked, told tales and wrote leaflets.

If I write about narrative these days, as well as engage in it, it's because, on my return journey to the East End, I recalled that the air was always thick with stories and the mealtimes were loud with them.

103

You can pin on me the neat label of scholarship boy if you like, but before you tidy me away into that stereotype and ask me to be grateful, remember that I had more than one schooling, my elementary school, my grammar school, the university, the Communist Party and, as I slowly came to realise, that vibrant academy, the Jewish East End. Jane is right. I am a hybrid.

A Necessary Myth:
Cable Street Revisited

Nothing is more fully agreed than the certainty that memory fails. Memory fails, leaving blanks, and fails by filling blanks mistakenly... But memory also succeeds. It succeeds enormously and profoundly; for it is fundamental to human life, not to say synonymous with it. (Karen Fields, 1989, p. 44)

In an issue of *Changing English* in 1996 I discussed autobiographical memory, a neglected topic, only recently given sustained attention by a few psychologists (Rubin, 1986; Conway, 1990). By a happy accident of sorts I can now supplement that with what I hope will be a useful addendum. Before I do so, here are the main propositions I advanced.

- Where and when we remember, the socio-cultural location, affects how we remember.
- A so-called 'flashbulb' memory, supposedly the bright, perfectly remembered moment, often turns out to be wrongly remembered and endowed with significance after the event or even before it.

I wrote then,

> While it is readily acknowledged and supported by copious evidence that there exists a class of memories which are particularly vivid, such memories, however, are not uniquely recorded. What makes them different is the high level of emotion which saturated the original experience and its meaning in the life of the rememberer... they prove to be peculiarly resistant to change; they achieve a canonical form which seems to render them proof against amnesiac loss. (Rosen, 1996, p. 24)

Halbwachs (1992) argued that all memory is in various ways collective memory, and he was counterposing this to the prevailing view that autobiography is essentially personal, emerging from the individual's psyche.

I was invited by *Marxism 1997,* an extensive progamme of lectures and discussions, to fill a slot entitled 'I was there', in which someone who had participated in an event which the left perceives to be a significant part of its history gives his/her testimony, brushing history against the grain, perhaps. The topic which was proposed for me was Cable Street, or perhaps I should say 'Cable Street' for reasons which will emerge. I agreed without hesitation. I had lived with Cable Street buzzing in some corner of my head for 60 years. More than that, I had let it take flight on innumerable occasions in conversations of all kinds in which I used my story to make a political point, to polish my credentials, perhaps, or quite simply to put into words an experience which is encircled by a particular aura. There was, too, the fact that I had for years been interested in all kinds of autobiographical practices and in autobiographical memory. Here was an instance which was in many ways a paradigm case — a memory which had been verbalised by me up to this point only in spontaneous speech, which I was about to revisit in a particular form, an address in an auditorium, certainly spoken, but this time supported by very full notes. Lastly the Cable Street event is one which I cherish, though I am aware that it has undergone transformation over the years and that it is, supremely, a kind of memory that has been and still is shared by others. The intensely personal and the publicly acknowledged merge to make something that is indelibly recorded.

Cable Street is a red letter day in the left-wing almanac that could teach us a lot about, first, how such occasions enter the consciousness as oppositional memory; second, what happens to such memories over time as intervening history puts a different gloss on them and; third, what, if anything, we do with them. A short while before I gave my talk I read a newly published book *Children of the Revolution* (Cohen, 1997), which is a compilation of autobiographical pieces. These were recollections of growing up in communist families. The title of the book itself tells us something about how the lexicon of the left requires its own little dictionary. None of the families in the book were, in fact, involved in a revolution, but, as they would have seen it, they were part of The Revolution: a very different matter indeed, a sustained process which would ultimately lead to a radical transformation of society. One of the writers, Pat Divine, says 'My father was the East London organiser of the party at the time of Cable Street' (Cohen, 1997, p. 79). Another, Jude Bloomfield, says, 'My father was a steward on the famous Cable Street march' (Cohen, 1997, p. 66). Neither of these writers thinks it necessary to explain what Cable Street was. Each confidently assumes that half a century after the event most readers of the book will get the reference which is enough to confer militant credentials on their fathers, especially as these comments are made *en passant*. One of them gets it a bit wrong: Cable Street was not a march but a blockade.

In the year before the 'I was there' talk I went to a commemoration of the Cable Street events at Gardiners Corner, because it was there on 4 October 1936 that a huge crowd had assembled to bar the way to Mosley's British Union of Fascists, who were proposing to march along the Jewish East End's major thoroughfare, Whitechapel Road: a blatant provocation. Gardiners Corner, therefore, was the proper assembly point for a commemoration meeting and march, 60 years after the event. Strangely, I remember asking myself for the very first time what should have been an obvious question. Why do we call it Cable Street? After all, the decisive happening was the gathering of a vast crowd at Gardiners Corner, where they solidly blocked five important roads which converged on a large open space. The answer seemed obvious to me once I had asked the question. It was in Cable Street that a barricade was constructed. A barricade! That potent icon of urban revolution: 1848 across Europe, the Parisian Communards in 1871, the Russian Revolution. So then, the very choice of name was a crucial part of the creation of a myth in the particular sense that I am giving to that word.

I went to the 60th anniversary of Cable Street and joined the damp little gathering. After a few speeches, off we went and I retraced some of the topography of my childhood and adolescence — Commercial Road, Cannon Street Road and, yes, Cable Street. We passed the end of New Road, a hundred or so yards from what had been my home in Nelson Street. Sadly, but I suppose inevitably, it was a thin turn-out. Any little rave-up could attract a larger gathering. Those who had 'been there' were invited to take a place of honour at the head of the demo. It turned out to be a dozen of us at most. I know, just from my own circle, it could easily have been more. That's the way of it. Memories of events which are not nurtured by state panoply struggle for a niche in people's consciousness. Yet, as I've indicated, Cable Street is still a name to be conjured with. Oral historians sometimes warn that if someone does not hurry along with a microphone in hand and interview a certain octogenarian a piece of history will die, which may well be true. But Cable Street still lives in the heads not only of people like me but of my relatively young audience. It has even found its way into the written record, into photos and film.

If you are lucky, there are moments in your life which are especially and uniquely illuminated. They stand out from the rest of your life as bright icons, huge representative symbols, which give meaning to how you have lived. This is why we purify such moments, polish them and, in our heads, play them over again and again. Cable Street was one of those moments for the left in the 1930s. We gave it a mythological and heroic dimension. Because we are short of such out and out victories, we badly needed those dynamic images.

I was 16 at the time and thoroughly demo-hardened from a very early age because I had grown up in a Jewish communist/socialist family. By Cable Street time I'd been on so many demos they were almost a way of life. Sometimes they were what they call these days 'a peaceful protest' and sometimes they were bloody confrontations. You could read from the faces of the police when you started out which would be which. Cable Street was bloody. I have wondered many times since precisely what demos are for. Do they make converts? When do they actually make a difference? Who takes notice? How do you measure success or failure? No doubt someone has analysed demos, done a sociology Ph.D. on the subject — 'The demonstration as a form of political action'. I have felt for a long time that whatever the declared function, the most important one is what it does for the participants — showing the flag, enjoying the collectivity, savouring in a particular way the solidarity of the occasion. Solidarity, of course, was always a key word in the lexicon.

Cable Street was, however, intended to be a demo with a difference. We were not going to plod through the streets to demand something or other. Quite simply, we told ourselves, we were going to stop the Fascists. How? With our bodies, as it turned out. There had to be enough of us to cram the huge space at Gardiners Corner and the streets that converged on it to ensure that Mosley's Blackshirts would not be able to pass. 'No pasaran!' they were saying in Spain.

As I remember it — have always remembered it — there were four of us, two couples, in fact, all close friends at 16, all at grammar schools, all Jewish. Two of that foursome still survive. Ask me by what precise social mechanism we arrived on the scene and I don't know the answer. Leaflets and posters perhaps, talk at home in my case, words exchanged in daily encounters. What I want, and perhaps need, to believe in order to keep the grandeur of the myth alive is that the East End was agog with it, that on everyone's lips was the news that Mosley was going to march and that we were going to stop him. Even the dozy Jewish authorities had roused themselves from their torpor, but only to pronounce that the Jewish people should stay at home and rebuff the Fascists with silent dignity. How often had we heard that from the old folk, 'Don't draw attention to yourselves. Don't make trouble. *Shtumm.*' This time they were only a bleat in the background.

By the time we arrived a seething crowd had already assembled, packed more and more tightly in all five roads. Right in the very centre was a tram whose driver had deliberately abandoned it. We knew we weren't going to a picnic but we weren't sure what exactly we were going to. There were police everywhere. I paint them for myself now as all grim-faced and menacing. Demo participants know that strange amalgam of emotions on such occasions. At the beginning we were caught up in a wild sense of excitement laced with naive optimism. This was going to be an instant victory. Kids that we were we thought we were freely enrolled in a spontaneous uprising. We shouted slogans and raised our clenched fists. A carnivalesque moment.

Hardly more than a moment, though, for the police had decided they could batter a way through for Mosley with baton charge after baton charge. This ceaseless onslaught went on for what seems now like hours. The pattern was unchanging: mounted police hitting out indiscriminately and the foot police following up to arrest the wounded, some bloody-headed. My little group was not in the front line. We were — less heroically — some 20 rows back on the Aldgate East side, swept to and fro by the unpredictable surges in the crowd. The police were operating from a space they had cleared right in the middle of Gardiners Corner. I suspect I know that only from photos I've seen since. I want to believe now that there was not a moment in the confrontation when we thought the police would succeed in smashing a way through. Finally, they must have recognised this when they negotiated with Mosley and he agreed to drop his original grandiose plan. He accepted a humbling alternative — a march along a back-street route — Cable Street, in fact. Of course, we didn't know about that at the time.

Somehow the word got round, 'All to Cable Street'. For those interested in the texture of everyday political action or, as I am sure some would put it, 'mob behaviour', how does that happen? Who breathed it into our ears and how did they know? I have no visual or auditory memory of getting the message, but I know that I did because of what followed. When I tried to answer those questions, looking back over so many years, I have to answer that it was not as I thought some radical magic at work conjuring up a brilliant inexplicable communication system (spontaneity again) but that the Communist Party had mounted a flexible military operation, a predetermined strategy. What mattered to us then was that we knew if we wanted to be where the action was we had to get to Cable Street, and then the word had it that in Cable Street there was a barricade, the barricade that later became famous. If that can still intoxicate the left today, imagine how it drove us on with wild imaginings. There might even be someone with a red flag and a blood-stained bandage round his forehead. If this wasn't The Revolution, it was the next best thing. A rare glorious victory was unfolding. So we were off.

Our naiveté now strikes me as comic. We didn't even ask ourselves the crucial question: how do you make sure you're on the right side of the barricade? Being on the wrong side of the barricades is an old metaphor snatched from revolutionary history and used less glamorously to mean siding with the class enemy in contemporary disputes. That the old metaphor should take a literal significance on the day is what strikes me as comic. Well, you can't stop a fellow demonstrator and ask, 'What's the best way to our side of the barricade, comrade?', even if you perceived it as a problem, which we didn't. Remember, I knew Cable Street very well, ever since my communist mother had dragged me as a very small boy to branch meetings in a shabby room reached across a dank yard in Cable Street.

Two of us, my girlfriend and I, made our way to the barricade. And there it was, on our left. We hugged ourselves.

111

An alien historic structure had become naturalised. Once again, we assumed that the righteous indignation of the masses had conjured it into being. Some folk had even overturned a lorry and consolidated the barricade with assorted junk. Intoxicated by the wonder of it, it took us a moment or two to realise that we were indeed in an absurd predicament. We had just enough time to take in the fact that to our right a row of mounted police filled the street from side to side and were just starting to trot, as a preliminary to the actual charge. We were stranded in front of some very small terraced houses which gave straight on to the pavement. Terrified, we pressed ourselves into a shallow doorway, hoping that the charge would sweep past us. The heroic version wasn't supposed to be like this. Suddenly the door behind us opened, hands grabbed us and pulled us inside.

That's really the end of my story because I recall nothing of what happened after that. The rescuing hands inscribed the last line, the perfect closure, my sense of an ending. I remember nothing of our talk with our rescuers, nothing of how and when we emerged, nothing of how we finally learned that we had won or what we did to celebrate.

That is how Cable Street took shape in my head through numerous informal tellings. Now it was being re-formed in a talk to a large and totally left-wing audience, whose presence, needless to say, was reshaping my story. Finally, there is this written prose version.

Let me now stand back from those versions and the satisfactions and perhaps self-indulgent pleasures that I have derived from them and see whether there is something to learn from them. All memory is inherently revisionist, as Freud put it, and, as Samuel and Thompson (1990, p. 8) write,

> Memory requires a radical simplification of its subject matter. All recollections are told from a standpoint in the present. In telling they need to make

sense of the past. That demands a selecting, order-
ing, and simplifying, a construction of a coherent
narrative whose logic works to draw the life story
towards the fable.

A short while after I had given my talk I met one of the
foursome who, in my version, went together to Gardiners
Corner and she told me very firmly that I was wrong. She
and her boyfriend (later her husband) were indeed there
but not with us. This accounts for the fact that by the time
of the barricade episode there were only two of us. It seems
a trivial error now, but I do not think it was. The foursome
for me is an important part of the myth. We remained life-
long socialist friends, and our mythic presence is about the
shared excitements of being young and collectively
enrolled in the purity of the Good Old Cause. I needed to
insert that enduring foursome as a significant little group,
separate from, but part of, that epic gathering. As I have
noted, my memory tells me that at the time I was euphoric
with what I felt was the spontaneity of the coming
together of that vast crowd. I did not have an inkling that
it was a highly organised affair and that the Communist
Party had set up a command post from which it did its best
to conduct the battle. It even had its own intelligence service. Years and years later I learned that a certain Hugh
Faulkner was a plant in Mosley's HQ and that he was able
to channel vital information as the day unfolded. I met
him as a fellow student at University College London, and
naturally he never breathed a word about his dangerous
mission. The tram at a standstill in the midst of the battle
has become, inevitably, a glittering object in most
accounts, both in its bright specificity and in the elevation
of the driver's bold act of solidarity. Dave Renton, who has
researched these events, tells me that he has met numerous people, each of whom claims to be the one who persuaded the driver to leave the tram!

Whatever else in my story changed over the years, it
always stopped at the identical point: the anonymous hands

pulling us into the shelter of the little terraced house. A constructed narrative is designed to deliver meaning, and a dramatic closure is a crucial part of the process. My podium telling, which is very much what I have written here, was a new version. It embodies for the first time post-event awarenesses, which have not hitherto been incorporated and which derive from some years of study of autobiographical memory and its mythological propensities. I must stress that I do not mean by this that I have so far transformed, rearranged and inflated Cable Street as to have distorted it out of its real significance and in defiance of what is now well-established knowledge of what happened on that day. However, what it used to be in my settled canonical form was a tale from a mythical golden age of anti-fascist militancy, untarnished by shabbiness and opportunism. The rescuing hands, my own story, were my own symbol of solidarity, but they belonged beyond doubt alongside the tramdriver, who was everybody's story. Cable Street happened, and thousands of ordinary folk did actually stop a fascist march from taking place in an unprecedented manner: the East End was never the same again. It was a time when the shadow of fascism hung over the whole of Europe. Jean Peneff (1990, p. 41), studying myth in life-stories, warns oral historians to be highly sceptical,

> The life-story can be a way of excusing ourselves in public, an effective means of building an enhanced self-image.

and

> ...by concentrating the story on the occupation of a factory, the celebration, or the meeting, the narrators turn their eyes away from what goes on behind the scenes.

Peneff is at the extreme pole of scepticism (for instance, 'We all to a greater or lesser extent falsify our social origins'!) She does not acknowledge that the storyteller may in fact not know what went on behind the scenes, which was the case in my story. She goes on to say that autobiography is one way in which we convince ourselves

> ...that the commitment, with all that lost time and energy, had a meaning, either individual — in the building of an interesting life — or collective; that history has a meaning. In the myth the trials are reversed: lost strikes become victories, failures only temporary and meaningful for the future. (p. 40)

I find it strange that Peneff does not see that mythical versions have their own kind of truth and that past commitments may indeed have the meaning which tellers believe them to have. Elizabeth Tonkin (1990), writing in the same volume, looks at the mythical element in our stories of personal experience, in a quite different, even opposed, manner.

> Myth is a representation of the past which historians recognise but generally as an alternative to proper history. All understandings of the past affect the present. Literate or illiterate, we are our memories. We try to shape our futures in the light of past experiences — or what we understand to have been past experiences — and representing how things were, we draw a social portrait which is a reference list of what to follow and what to avoid. The model is part of the processes we live in and call 'groups', 'institutions' and 'society' and it helps to reproduce or modify them. (p. 25)

One of the key turning points in my thinking about autobiography was provided by the work I have now cited several times, *The Myths We Live By* (Samuel and Thompson, 1990), and in particular by the editors' introduction (pp. 1-21). I owe much of my present understanding of the Cable

115

Street story to their volume. It taught me the many ways in which stories of our pasts are to a greater or lesser extent myths. It also represented a turning point for oral historians in the way they regarded the materials they collected.

> When we listen now to a life-story, the manner of its telling seems to us as important as what is told... it has also brought a new and much broader potential. As soon as we recognise the value of the subjective in individual testimonies we challenge the accepted categories of history. We reintroduce the emotionality, the fears and fantasies carried by the metaphors of memory, which historians have been so anxious to write out of their accounts... each individual story draws on a common culture: a defiance of the rigid categorisation of private and public, just as of memory and reality. (p. 2)

All students of autobiography draw attention to its fictive features, but Samuel and Thompson, in presenting a rich and challenging way of looking at oral memory, are at pains to insist that they are not working with memories of a false past, that much of what is delivered in oral testimony, especially its rich detail, 'remains objectively valid, sometimes demonstrably so from other sources' (p. 6). Oral memory, they go on to claim, has a double validity, in which 'myth was embedded in real experience: both growing from it and helping to shape its perception'. I now see the Cable Street story in this light. I am sure that there have been and still are thousands of stories of Cable Street in circulation which each express a participant's necessary myth. Put them together, and collectively they express a larger necessary myth, magnifying an event which was a speck on the political map of 1936 into a decisive turning-point which, in a modest way, it was.

I have only this to add. Autobiographical practices in various guises have found their way into the curriculum at every level of education, chiefly through forms of 'changing English' from the 1960s onwards. The most innovative element has been the involvement of students in recording their own, their families' and their communities' memories. All this activity could now include considerations of the mythical elements in these stories. Everywhere there are Cable Streets in local memory, which need to be evoked, valued and scrutinised thoughtfully and positively.

References

Cohen, P. (1997) *Children of the Revolution* (London, Lawrence and Wishart).
Conway, M.A. (1990) *Autobiographical Memory* (Buckingham, Open University Press).
Fields, K. (1989) What one cannot remember mistakenly, *Oral History Journal*, 17:1, Spring, pp. 44-53.
Halbwachs, M. (1992) *Collective Memory* (Chicago, University of Chicago Press).
Peneff, J. (1990) Myths in life-stories, in: R. Samuel & P. Thompson (Eds) *The Myths We Live By* (London, Routledge).
Rosen, H. (1996) Autobiographical memory, *Changing English*, 3: 1, pp. 21-34.
Rubin, D.C. (1986) (Ed.) *Autobiographical Memory* (Cambridge, Cambridge University Press).
Samuel, R. & Thompson, P. (Eds) (1990) *The Myths We Live By* (London, Routledge).
Tonkin, E. (1990) History and the myth of realism, in: Samuel, R. & Thompson, P. (Eds) *The Myths We Live By* (London, Routledge).

A Necessary Myth first appeared in *Changing English*

For Beatrice Hastings

It was a most unlikely assignation with a lady at her flat in Belsize Park. I was twelve, perhaps a bit more, and she must have been fiftyish. I was not relishing this encounter mostly because I did not understand why it was happening, not for sure anyway. She wore long blood-red earrings which were never still. Beatrice. A very gentile name. I didn't at the time know anyone called Beatrice. There was Great-aunt Beatty who may have been Beatrice on her birth certificate but I didn't know about that. Just like there were Aunt Addie who was really Adelaide and Aunt Lallie who was Sarah and Aunt Millie who was Amelia and my *booba* Betsy who was Betsy. It seemed to us at home that Beatrice Hastings was properly so-called and her name alone kept her at arm's length in spite of her not infrequent appearances to eat and talk with us in our sombre brown kitchen.

"Beatrice Hastings said she liked my *borsht*," *booba* said. "I don't believe it. Like Bella Stern saying she liked my cheesecake. She'd say she liked it if I gave her poison. That's their way."

"*Borsht* or no *borsht*," said my *zeider*, "Beatrice Hastings is a comrade. To be a comrade you're not obliged to like *borsht*."

But even I knew it would have helped.

"Beatrice Hastings," he went on, has... has... well... come over."

Like the rest of us, his classification system couldn't quite place her. I think if it hadn't been for the comrade bit he could have sorted it out. But then, if it hadn't been for the comrade bit he wouldn't have needed to.

I surfaced at Belsize Park underground station on the Northern Line. I'd never got out there before. It all looked alien, perhaps hostile, and on that November late afternoon it was slightly foggy and dampish. The shops were too smart for my liking, none of them spilling onto the pavement, not a *schlepper* in sight, and the passers-by far too well-dressed. They weren't hanging about in twos or threes to have a *muttel*, shaking and nodding their heads, expecting people to edge their way round them. They were going about their affairs in a very direct eyes-ahead sort of way.

"Your petit-bourgeois," said my Uncle Sam (who knew his Marxist alphabet from *Anti-Duhring* to *Zinoviev*) "doesn't like the streets, too unpredictable and teeming with proletarians with bombs in their pockets."

The petit-bourgeois on Haverstock Hill didn't seem the least bit bothered by all that. Inside their thick overcoats and fur collars they looked very much at home. I wasn't. I slouched towards Beatrice Hastings's flat, baffled by this sortie over the border not of my choosing. Somehow I found my way across the main road and along Belsize Avenue, then into Belsize Park Gardens. Did I have a map? Had I learned the name and route by heart? No *A to Z* that's for sure. Since that moment now tastes of uncertainty and timidity I wonder about such things. Perhaps I was less of a *nebbich* than I have imagined.

Belsize Park Gardens was a street of sudden quiet gentility, huge stuccoed Victorian fortresses with great windows, porticoes with columns, barred basements and substantial walls. I found the house. I found the right bell-push next to a handwritten 'Beatrice Hastings'. There was nothing for it. I rang the bell and waited shakily. Ring a doorbell, rap a knocker, rattle a letterbox, bang on the woodwork and always there will be that second or two of anxiety or hope before you cross the threshold from everyone's street to the private indoors. Sure, I could have fled and told my mother I couldn't find the house or something, but for all my unwillingness and resentful spirit there was also, lurking deep down, a smatch of excitement and promise. It was just possible that, in spite of the inevitable torment of the coming *tête-a-tête*, something special and good for me would emerge.

I suppose I'd better go back a bit before I go up into the flat and tell about what happened. The thing is, if I were speaking the story this would be the moment when I would say 'Half a minute. I forgot to tell you...' Nobody would mind. They'd let you mend and patch as you go. They'd even help you out if need be. 'Great Uncle Schmul,' someone will say, telling the tale once more of how he got to England and thought it was America, 'used to live in the Portobello Road after the Boer War. Master tailor he was.' 'Great Uncle Schmul? No, no,' says Aunt Millie 'A tailor? Just a little furrier in Ladbroke Grove. After the Boer War, like you say. How come he lived up West?' Just putting the record straight. No hard feelings. So I'll go back.

My *zeider* began it. He was given to bringing home out of the blue people he'd run into, we never knew how. They were always in our eyes exotics, collectors items, you might say, real finds. There was the improbably Hedley, for instance, whom *Zeider* had met down in the docks. And what was *Zeider* doing in that dangerous and hostile territory? Something political, we guessed vaguely. Hedley was a black seaman from Jamaica, I think. This was the Thirties, remember. Not many Hedleys about then. I marvelled at my *booba* who always kept a watchful eye on the food supply. To my surprise and her credit she didn't bat an eyelid. She was a stern and judgmental woman and didn't exactly smother Hedley with hospitality. He was not in her *gas-in-shtetl* class but she always found him a place and a plate at the kitchen table. The neighbours monitored his toings and froings, wild with curiosity and churning with suspicions.

"*Gottinue!* A *schvartzer*! That Betsy Hyams, don't I know she doesn't keep *kashrus*? So what do you expect? And that Joe Hyams (my *zeider*) he's always *kreerching* round meetings. On *shabbas* even. Meetings, meetings. Where else would he find a *schvartzer*? In *schul*, I suppose."

They prophesied disaster. "They're all *gonovim*. He'll take everything one day."

121

From time to time, when Hedley's ship was in dock, he'd show up at the house bringing with him food, mostly big root crops we could not recognise, never seen in Hessel Street market. I think the family relished their display of comradely broadmindedness, but food they did not know put this to the severest of tests.

Booba turned over a big turnipish-potatoish lump in her hands, frowned and put it away on the dresser. Hedley laughed his head off, knowing exactly what was going on. He peeled and scraped and chopped, beamed over a saucepan and brewed until a dark brown liquid swirled round his gift. We all knew that we could do no less than give it a try. It tasted worse than the most punitive medicine. We did what we always did thereafter, gritted our teeth, gulped and did not gag. After all, Hedley had to do the same when he bravely tackled pickled herring. The thing is that we, the kids that is, liked Hedley because he laughed more than all the grown-ups put together. He could make it seem as though he had pulled off the top joint of his thumb and he taught me how to do it. *Zeider* loved these occasions. He hugged himself,

"He's a *mensch*, a real *mensch*," and we agreed.

Of course he was proving something. No harm in that.

When Hedley left, Mrs Hamburger, prompt on her doorstep, sourly saw him off the street and the Kromlechs, crammed goggle-eyed in their doorway, waited till he came abreast to slam the door, surprised, I suppose, that we had not yet been murdered in our beds.

"Who's that blackie who comes round your house?" Herbie next door asked. I laughed in his face.

"A captain. A pirate captain. My *zeider's* been on his ship and seen the skull and crossbones."

Herbie wasn't laughing but he stopped asking me about Hedley.

My mother easily caught the habit of bringing home non-ghetto strangers, mostly *goyim*. One day she arrived with a tall blonde sailor from Hamburg who was a member of the German Communist Party, the KPD. He wasn't her own find but had been passed on by the comrades. I was excited by a little transaction which used to take place in the hallway when he came, a transaction which I realized or imagined was illicit. My mother either collected from him, or gave him, I can't remember which, a batch of contraband copies of a journal which she called *In-Pre-Core*, a name so impenetrable that it made me even more sure that there was something very risky and subversive afoot, especially as it was printed on very thin slippery paper like the pages of the *Concise Oxford*. It was years before I found out that it was *International Press Correspondence*, one of the Comintern's enterprises, no less. Kurt came from time to time for his pick-ups or drops. He was quiet and uneasy and not having much English didn't help but the grown-ups managed fairly well with transmogrified Yiddish and there was a certain amount of sport as they sorted out who meant what. From time to time Kurt looked utterly baffled but Lallie wasn't to know that '*machatonim*' wasn't a German word. Sometimes Kurt went off for furtive mutterings with my mother which must have stretched her Yiddish-German to the limit. *Booba* fed him but eyed him sternly and warily. Still, she always tried to find him a bit of wurst to put on the table, believing this would console him for being away from home. His visits became less and less frequent and then he stopped coming altogether. Hitler had come to power. We did not dare say to each other what we thought. I imagined that *In-Pre-Core* had done for him and I saw him being manhandled by a uniformed thug which *In-Pre-Core* tumbled onto the pavement from under his arm. One day somebody mentioned Kurt's name and my mother wept.

There were others, too, until we were almost used to these arrivals, so unlike those uncles and aunts and cousins who sat for hours over tea and *kichelech* or the excitable tailors with their talk of the impending doom of capitalism and the next demo. But I wasn't ready for Beatrice Hastings. As outlandish as Hedley and Kurt were, they slid into the cramped kitchen in Nelson Street and installed themselves around the old wooden table quite easily. *Booba* handled Hedley's roots with aplomb compared with her dismay at Beatrice Hastings's little oval tins of vegetarian something-or-another and her nut cutlets. Beatrice Hastings was our first vegetarian but she didn't win a single convert in our house. The tins contained pastes of unspeakable mid-brown or yellow colours and unidentifiable odours and tastes. Our courtesies didn't rise to this. Only my mother made a bold pretence of feeding happily with her guest. When Beatrice Hastings nodded away *Booba's kreplech* soup, a legend in the family, we scored this up as a black mark.

"She's only a high class *shiksa*," *Booba* said. "Never done a hand's turn for herself. Surrounded by *tuchas lechers* and low-lives. And she brings me those tins of *dreck*. And I'll tell you something else. Been through a few men in her day. She's probably got one hanging around somewhere right now."

My mother and *Zeider* looked at each other like conspirators and *Zeider* mouthed "*shtumm*."

I watched those blood red earrings jiggling to the vibrations of her voice. And what a voice! I may have heard one or two like it on the wireless or in the newsreels but I had never had one aimed straight at me from a yard away, emerging from a totally organised face. It wasn't just posh. Miss Drysdale, one of my teachers, talked posh and Henriques, boss of the Jewish boys' club, talked posh but this was born-to-rule super-posh, Bloomsbury posh, Roedean posh. It was the voice of someone who never expected to be gainsaid. Her hair was steely grey, straight, fringed over the forehead and clipped sharply below the ears. It was a style which my son, decades later, spotting certain older anti-nuclear women on the march, called Aldermaston hair. East End ladies of this era had their own notions of decent middle-aged style and they didn't run to minimalism. As for Beatrice Hastings's clothes, they seemed to us neither tailored nor dress-made, essential requirements at the hub of the rag trade. We couldn't place these garments which hung loosely and were made from rough folky fabrics with shaky stripes in dark browns, purples and deep reds. She never wore a hat. We did eventually break bread together but I fancy she was not quite ready for seeded rye and black bread. Give her her due, she managed well enough. No doubt she came from a long line of ladies who took free soup to poor cottagers and expected to venture into quarters utterly remote from their own and, if need be, in any part of the world. Don't misunderstand me, there wasn't a whiff of this in her demeanour. On the contrary, she believed she could learn something from my mother and *Zeider*. I'm only saying that part of her inheritance had taught her to be quite unabashed by our alien ways and our outside lavatory.

There was always a certain twitchiness in the room, not out of nervous deference but because we just didn't know what we had to do to reach across the gulf between us, even though she was a comrade. *Zeider* talked much less and his bonhomie evaporated. He fidgeted when she looked at him and he rolled a lot of cigarettes. *Booba* was totally silent and I was suddenly very aware of her little gold earrings and the tigerclaw brooch with its gold mounting and her white hair stretched tautly in a bun (no *sheitel*) and her dark workaday pinafore. She resisted conversation.

"Were you born here, Mrs Hyams?"

"No."

"Really? Where then?"

"Newcastle."

Newcastle! I didn't expect that. Some of my father's people lived in Gosforth. *Booba* looked very slightly cross.

My mother, knowing that all was not going well, tried to salvage something from the afternoon.

"Beatrice," she said, "have you always been a journalist?"

"Good God, no! I'm not a real one now. Don't think I've ever actually done an honest job in my life. Honest jobs don't run in the family. Too much money about. Once did

125

a bit of auxiliary nursing till I realized I was acting the Lady Bountiful."

I was taking notice now. Journalist. Clever woman. My first real writer. What did she write? Would we see some of her stuff? My mother surely must have read some of it.

Things got better between us so we saw a lot more of her, against all the odds, almost taking her into the family with her veggie tins. *Booba* stopped glowering. Where could my mother possibly have found her? It turned out they had found themselves on a march to Hyde Park and got talking, as happens. There was ragged slogan shouting, of course — hands off this, smash that, free somebody, fight something and Beatrice Hastings confessed she felt embarrassed marching through the West End with the *sans-culottes*. Bellowing slogans was completely beyond her because bellowing of any kind just wasn't in her repertoire.

"How do you do it without feeling a bit of an ass?" she had asked.

"I've been doing it for so long I don't know," said my mother who then patiently explained about party discipline. "Don't worry about it. You're here, aren't you? That's the big thing. It'll come. I used to think I'd never work up the nerve to sell the *Daily Worker* at Aldgate East Station. Even for Lenin it must have been embarrassing at first. Anyway, it's harder for us women."

They ended up taking tea in Lyons Corner House at Marble Arch. Eventually my mother lured her onto a committee which organised womens' conferences on birth control.

Undoubtedly they hit it off. Beatrice Hastings had been swept to the Communist Party like others in the thirties who moved across from good causes. She was now not only a comrade and fellow reader of the *Daily Worker* but also a catch. For all my mother's impeccable communist credentials and her hammer and sickle red star badge, I have to say she bathed in Beatrice Hastings's aura of confidence, education and (need I say it?) wealth. She was in

126

this light a superior woman to be paraded before the family as my mother's social achievement. Beatrice Hastings was full of books and papers, some of which she would leave on the kitchen table as she left. I tried to read one of them, Samuel Butler's *The Way of All Flesh* and the joke is that my mother already had a copy with a broken spine and dog-eared pages, tucked away in her little bookcase. She knew a lot of people whose names were in the papers. When she spoke about the Royal Family her opinions seemed to have been formed when dining with them.

"Them," she once snorted, "dogs and horses, the only things they know about."

And then it turned out she had been the mistress, as they used to say, of a well-known editor of a radical journal, who still has a modest niche in encyclopaedias. She herself started a little lefty weekly as if there weren't enough already to go round, My mother showed me an issue or two.

"She writes every line herself," she said, keeping a straight face.

It had about four grey pages of double columns. I don't think she made much of an effort to sell it. It was more of a kind of accessory, like a good quality handbag. I don't mean to mock her, for the truth is I was dazzled by this *grande dame* who, I had to admit reluctantly, knew more than my mother about some things. Once, finding me doing my French homework and discovering that my pronunciation was barbaric, she set about improving it. Caught in such august attention, I prayed she would soon give up for my words stuck in my throat. She did. On the other hand, when foreign place names came up in all the political talk, she made me look them up in an atlas — Brest-Litovsk, Locarno, Manchukuo, Amritsar. I felt noticed.

I might have simply added Beatrice Hastings to my collection of folk who, for a few precious hours, made the kitchen exciting and provided us with endless gossip. I might have been left with no more than a few bright tableaux of Beatrice Hastings, looking for instance, incredulously at a Yiddish newspaper while *Zeider* translated the hieroglyphics and coming near to permitting herself to look surprised, shocked even, when she discovered that we, atheists all, not only did the complete *seder* night at the beginning of Passover and relished it but even stopped eating bread. She wasn't ready for the dozens of boxes of *matzos* and trays of eggs piled high on the landing.

"If this is what atheist Jews do, what's left for the orthodox ones?"

"The synagogue," said *Zeider*.

A few bright images, no more, if that's all there had been to it. But then there came the day when my mother, after a few obscure hints, let me understand that I was going to visit Beatrice Hastings at her flat in Belsize Park. Perhaps I had been invited. Perhaps my mother had fished for it. Perhaps they had concocted the idea together, each thinking in her own way, it would do me some good. Some of the cultured life would brush off and I'd stop dropping aitches forever, be given an improving book or two and — who knows? — be taken out.

"Beatrice says four o'clock. For tea. You take the Underground to Belsize Park."

And then she added very slowly

"She wouldn't do this for anybody, you know."

More than my mother's words, it was her demeanour which told me she had high hopes for my *tête-a-tête*. It signalled weighty expectation. I was full of foreboding. Tea! Mustn't use my own teaspoon to take sugar from the bowl, mustn't put my helping of jam straight on the bread. Don't slurp, don't make munching noises. There must have been something I didn't yet know which would shame me. What would we talk about? I bet she'll ask me about school and I'll have to tell a few lies. How long must I stay? It was going to be an ordeal, without doubt, but all the same Beatrice Hastings might become my patron and I her *protégé*. It was frightening and thrilling.

I followed Beatrice Hastings up the carpeted stairs and

after her, brushed past the green baize draught curtain into a very large room. I didn't know one even faintly like it. Even Dr Abrams's, though it was big, was comfy and battered with a leaking sofa and lots of higgledy-piggledy books. My school friend, Harry Mintz, had a big sitting room over his parents' shop. It was crammed with furniture from side to side, all looking brand new. I never saw it in use. In our own house, apart from the kitchen, there was a small semi-basement living room almost filled by a large table, a dozen hard chairs and a basket armchair next to the kitchen for my *booba's* sole use. In Beatrice Hastings's room the heavy curtains, already drawn, hung from floor to ceiling. Several standard lamps cast pools of light on a thick, mostly red, carpet. The rest of the room was, to my eyes, in semi-darkness. In this tasteful cave I could see items of furniture and none of them matched. I could just make out that the walls were lined with bookcases and somewhere there were shelves with a dinner service on display. I stepped into the room carefully. I was given a seat by a little table under one of the lamps.

"Tea would be good," said Beatrice Hastings, "don't you think? Do you like muffins? Better than crumpets, lighter. Dripping with butter, eh?"

"Yes, yes," I said. 'Yes, please."

Any other time I would have been licking my chops at the thought of it. Dripping with butter? Where will the drips go?

She left the room and came back holding a tray with curvy edges and on it frighteningly delicate china. I prepared to take my test. But you lose marks for trying too hard, don't you? And I didn't know what to do about my buttery lips. I can't remember what we talked about but it wasn't about school. At one point she asked me if I'd ever been to Whitechapel Art Gallery. I hadn't but knew that I should have been. She nursed the conversation along, apparently not the least dismayed by my minimal responses, filling in with little stories about her childhood somewhere in the green shires and rebel escapades in her

129

hated boarding school. Sitting close by this completely composed lady and trying to find responses which wouldn't come while managing my tea-cup and muffin plate, I knew I had failed the conversation test. And me from a family where everyone, myself included, competed noisily for conversational space. I was, as the Australians say, duchessed. I imagined that my patron-elect could hardly wait to send me on my way back to Belsize Park Station, Whitechapel and her good friend, my mother.

Not a bit of it. When the tea things were cleared she turned to me.

"I'd like to show you some of my paintings. I've been trying out some new ideas. Would you like that?"

Well, you can't really refuse, can you? She permitted herself a tiny laugh from far down her throat. Another test now, I thought.

She brought into the room one of those huge artists' folders, untied the bows and began turning over the poster-size paintings one by one, very slowly. They were all on bright red matt paper and consisted of very avant-garde black whirls and twirls, twists and turns. I began slowly to realize that incorporated into each one and only just detectable was a black, very stylised, hammer and sickle. She sat there coolly turning the sheets and glancing up at me from time to time. I knew, of course, that some kind of bright perceptive remark was expected of me and I knew just as certainly that I had absolutely nothing to say. If she had been turning over the Mona Lisa, the Laughing Cavalier or the Stag at Bay I wouldn't have had anything to say either because I had no painting talk whatsoever. My silence was the more total because I actually thought in a kind of philistine way that the paintings were indecipherable rubbish and no more than the self-indulgence of an eccentric with too much time on her hands. This phase of the visit reduced me to such dumb misery that I had no thought but to count the minutes before I would be able to go.

So I failed. I know that and that all my far-fetched hopes

had dissolved over those silly paintings. But why do I recall that occasion so vividly that with the greatest of ease I can summon up that room and my excruciations in it? Humiliations bite deep and are terribly durable. But that's not it. I don't think I've mentioned that Beatrice Hastings was a very handsome woman and must have been a real beauty in her day. But when I had recovered from that wretched tea, young as I was, I realized that she was on her way down to join the has-beens. I admired her, might have loved her if she had been more accessible and, as *Zeider* had said, she was a comrade. So I was sad for her and even mourned her better times which I knew nothing about.

Beatrice Hastings was, however, no stranger to the Jewish world, having lived with the artist Amadeo Modigliani. Beatrice Hastings was also a model for Modigliani. She committed suicide in 1943.

Milchikke and Fleischikke

Cousin Bernie had something in mind. He always did. Why else would I catch the rickety tram almost every weekend, leave behind school friends and street friends and embrace of the Jewish East End? The tram rocked along ugly Commercial Street and crossed the invisible frontier into the (mostly) gentile world, past Shoreditch church and on to Kingsland Road in Dalston. I got off at the old fire station and went down a turning at the side of it where a few blocks away was Aunt Lallie's and Uncle Ike's house on a corner. Dalston at the time had, I believe, been a first staging post on the Jewish escape route from the ghetto. And it felt like it. Distinctly gentile. True, you could find a little synagogue here and there and, if you knew where, smoked salmon and cream cheese.

Uncle Ike could afford to buy his house in Dalston. At the time I couldn't take in the idea of buying a house. How did you so such a thing? All the families I knew had well-worn rent books and rent collectors haunted the streets like the school attendance officers and the gas board men. It was not so much the grand gesture of house buying which baffled me as the sheer incomprehensibility of the transaction. Buying and selling you did in shops and at market stalls all the time, mostly food, clothes and sweets. You put down your money and you got something over the counter. You nearly always haggled. Bating, it was called. The sale would appear to have broken down and the buyer would start walking away.

"Come back, you *schnorrer*. Make it fivepence?"

So what happened with houses? I hadn't the faintest idea.

Uncle Ike was an aristocrat of labour, as lefties would have said, a compositor at *Lloyd's Gazette*. I was given to understand that it was a classy occupation and it had put him into the house-buying bracket. The family used to name his job with a certain incredulous relish. That too was beyond me. What exactly did a compositor do? How did Uncle Ike end up in the City and escape the sweat shops? Where had he learned his trade, so different from the tailoring and all the other rag trade jobs? Mind you, my uncles-by-marriage and the other assorted family males were a somewhat non-standard collection — a long-distance lorry driver, a cheap men's wear shop owner, a sort of clerical worker (sometime furrier), manager of a flea-pit cinema. True, there was Uncle Jack with his huge multi-volume tailoring books which sat in a row like the *Encyclopaedia Britannica*. My own father had been a shoe-maker, a factory worker not a cobbler.

Uncle Ike was very well-to-do by our standards. His wages would have amounted to more than the precarious profits of Aunt Millie's and Uncle Alf's absolutely bottom of the market shop in the poverty of Hoxton Street Market. (Hoxton! I ask you.) It was easy for me to see that Bernie's house was a lot posher than ours back in the East End. Nothing grand, of course, solid early Victorian on the very edge of Georgian De Beauvoir Town. I searched it out recently after a lapse of well over sixty years. It was more modest than I remembered. I had in my memory given it a much more imposing front door but the railings were still there and the stone steps to the basement and what had once been a front garden. So different from our house which you stepped straight into from a narrow pavement and entered a mean dark corridor. The Dalston house was big enough for Bernie and me to lose ourselves in, to be out of earshot and get up to things. I can see now that at the age of eleven and twelve I might have been a bit too overawed to undertake my weekly trips on the rocking tram but, although there was plenty of furniture around, there was no three-piece-suite nor polished mahogany sideboard. It was well-worn but it was not shabby and battered. The arm chairs were for lolling in and Uncle Ike took his snory forty winks with his shoes on in a big settee. It always looked as though he had left the imprint of his body on it for ever. Nothing was kept for best or banned to kids.

I heard Aunt Millie say one day, 'Lallie is not *balabuste*. *Ay, ay*, that kitchen of hers!' and the sisters, sipping their lemon tea, all agreed. The Yiddish word meant no more than a good housewife. But when they said *balabuste* they meant much more. You could hear it in their voices. At the very least it meant not just competence but an assured flair in all matters domestic and, if possible, a speciality thrown in — an extra something in *kreplech*, an elusive flavour in the *lokschen* soup, the sponge *plaver* cake so light you could blow it away. Aunt Lallie wasn't going to get medals for anything of that kind. There were even suspicions about the proper maintenance of *kashrus*, keeping things kosher. When visitors appeared on the doorstep unexpectedly there were none of the obligatory reserves in the larder or the cellar, no home-made picked cucumbers, no chopped herring, no platters of calves' foot jelly, no cinnamon balls.

"Don't worry, don't worry," she'd say. "I'll send out for salt-beef sandwiches and gherkins." And that meant a *schlepp* all the way to Ridley Road.

"Bernie!" she'd shout opening her purse, "and while you're at it get some *platzels*."

"No, not bagels. His bagels are like rubber."

She didn't get agitated about a spot of *schmalz* here or there or a little scratch on the dining room table. You'd never see her dashing about devotedly with a polish cloth. I can hear her saying, 'Leave it, leave it. It'll be like that when I'm dead'. When her five sisters said that she was no *balabuste* they were being distinctly critical, but they were all as fond of her as I was. They saw in her an unruffled good nature and undemonstrative affection, which wasn't in their repertoire I can tell you. Surprisingly they appreciated her steadfast lack of malice and refusal to be drawn into their deadly vendettas and corrosive jealousies — Aunt Millie and Aunt Rene didn't speak to each for decades after some dispute. So I loved going to her house.

135

Though she always greeted me with a smile and a quick hug, she had abandoned the ritual smother of cuddles laced with interrogation and demands for obligatory affection.

I was drawn irresistibly to the Dalston house and cousin Bernie's plans for a good time. It seems to me now that, although the East End could wrap around you a kind of reassurance and the comfort of the familiar and was not without its excitements, over there there was a whiff of freedom. I would always begin to savour it when I passed Shoreditch Church. It may have been something else too. The house itself felt less Jewish. Yet my own close family had abandoned most of the orthodoxies. All the same you had to live Jewish; the most committed atheists wouldn't been seen eating bread during Passover. Where would they have bought it? What would good neighbours have made of it? No *mezuzzah* on the doorpost would have been unthinkable. I suppose there was one on the Dalston house though I wouldn't swear to it. There were no prayer books about and there was no Friday night business with big brass candlesticks and the *challah* loaf. Nevertheless, there were certain sticking points, to me completely arbitrary but probably not. To my surprise Aunt Lallie kept two sets of dishes so that milk and meat foods, *milchikke un fleischikke*, would never be served together nor eaten together. Thus the lemon tea at the end of meat meals. I don't think that for Aunt Lally all this had anything to do with God or specifically religious practices. A *balabuste* she might not be but she drew the line somewhere and saw her kitchen as a Jewish kitchen. If anyone looked like being a bit slipshod in putting away the dishes, she'd say with rare vehemence,

"Never, never, milk with meat; *milchikke* with *fleischikke* never!"

There was something a touch gentile about Uncle Ike. Part of it was his English (to me) quietness, reserve and self-control. I couldn't have imagined him in a praying shawl or walking around the house with his head covered

136

at all times. For all I know he may have been able to speak Yiddish like the rest of his generation but I never heard him doing so. However, he was not so secularized that he didn't go to synagogue on *Yom Kippur*, the Day of Atonement. He had his sins to wash away like all the other one-day-in-the-year attenders.

None of the taboo foods were ever brought into the house. Aunt Lally even went so far as to do a lot of her shopping in the East End — to be on the safe side, as she said, and to have a long *muttel* with her mother and sisters over tea and *plaver*. The branched candlestick for *Chanachah* was lit in the approved sequence. Births, marriages and deaths were fully observed with the old rituals. In spite of all that I was somewhat taken about when Bernie said to me one day,

"Guess what! I'm going to get *barmitzvahed* in the summer. I've been going to classes. I'm learning my portion to say in *schul*. You have to sing it all, you know. Funny tunes. Makes me a bit nervous."

"Sing!" I said, "not exactly a *chazan*, are you?"

In fact he was what my teacher would have called a grunter. Bernie was not the archetypal *barmitzvah* boy either. I know he hadn't dabbled in that kind of thing before. It was yet another notice to me that, when observance began to melt away or seemed in utter dissolution, there were some things which stood intact and inviolable. Bernie's announcement was made in such a matter-of-fact way that it was as though he'd said he was going to Brighton for the summer holiday. At the same time I sensed he was waiting for my response and perhaps was a bit anxious about it.

"What are you getting *barmitzvahed* for?"

"What for? What for? Because you do. You must, It's like getting married. And anyway, we're not *goyim*, are we?"

Realizing that didn't quite meet the case, he added,

"My *cheder* teacher says that once you're *barmitzvahed* you can be one of the *minyan* like a grown-up man."

What's he talking about? I thought. I knew what a *minyan* was from when my grandfather died. Every evening at our house a little quorum of ten assembled to say mourner's *Kaddish*, the prayers for the dead. You could step into the street and ask any passing male to make up the number.

"Better watch out," I said, "or someone will rush out into Balls Pond Road and grab you to make up the *minyan*. They're a bit short up there."

"Don't mock," said Bernie. "It's a serious thing. Once in a lifetime and only for boys."

I knew because once you reached a certain size the older folk, relatives and friends, would stop you in the street and ask, 'Are you *barmitzvahed* yet?'

"Do you know," said Bernie, and he laughed, "you can be called up in *schul* any time to read a portion of the law."

There was no risk of that as he never went to *schul*. His *barmitzvah* piece had to be learnt by rote because like me he couldn't read Hebrew even in its easier form, let alone the vowel-less *Torah* scroll.

"Anyway," said Bernie, "You get terrific presents. My dad's going to give me a gold wrist watch. And you get your first suit with long trousers."

Now he was scoring. I felt very excluded, especially as my very, very ideological mother had already made it quite clear that *barmitzvahs* were part of the opium of the masses. No portion of the law, presents and long trousers for me. The whole business, one way or another, was putting Bernie at arm's length, making him more East End than Dalston. He receded a little from the boy who, a year older than me, was always ready with the next exploit which might try Aunt Lallie's patience.

I'd always go along with it. Even rather tame notions took on a touch of daring. Was it his infectious, conspiratorial tone or the way he grabbed my arm to tug me towards adventure? How else could the condensed milk scheme have seduced me? The plan was no more than to buy a large tin of condensed milk and eat all of it between us. Silly really, but bear in mind that condensed milk was taboo, not because of any dietetic law but rather because of food snobbery. It came into the category of very cheap foods which were regarded as poverty fare, fit only for the desperately poor, and, whisper it, gentiles. After all, it said on the condensed milk tins "unfit for babies" and I had seen feckless mothers outside pubs dipping their babies' dummies in them. On the poverty list were pilchards, bargain price tinned peas (for some reason watery blue), flavourless pineapple chunks at fourpence ha'penny a tin and pallid meat loaf. Yet we had both tasted tinned milk somewhere or another and like millions of other kids we regarded it as a gift from the gods, proletarian ambrosia; thick, sticky, sweet. It lingered in the mouth. Top class nosh.

"What do we do," I asked, "spread it on bread?"

"Spread it on bread! You'd have to eat a whole loaf. No. We get a couple of spoons and eat it straight out of the tin. Every bit. As much as we want."

I was ready for this gross piggery though a bit anxious about our being found out. But we were away down the Kingsland Road and bought our condensed milk for pennies and then back to the house. By now I was greedily excited.

"Are they out?" I whispered.

"Gone to my uncle's. Won't be back for ages."

That was another attractive thing about the place. Aunt Lally and Uncle Ike would often go out leaving us on our own. They didn't sit about like the others, drinking tea or half dozing in armchairs or playing cards for hours. My cousin Herbie, Bernie's older brother, was usually about his own business unless he was doing his homework or he might be doing a grown-up job serving in Aunt Millie's shop in Hoxton. We often had the whole house to ourselves.

So we were safe with our condensed milk. We dived into the kitchen, opened the tin, got out our spoons and, our heads brushing together, started guzzling like pigs at a trough. It was all we had yearned for and we kept going. Very suddenly I was slowing down.

"I feel a bit sick," I said, "I've had enough."

"Me too," said Bernie. "But we've had a lot."

"What will we do with the rest?"

"Give it to the cat." said Bernie.

The cat clanked around the room and adroitly licked the can clean and then went off to see the world. We wrapped the can in newspaper and put it in the bin. We weren't exactly flush with success but we had come through, we thought. Then the grown-ups came home.

"Cat's been sick," said Aunt Lallie, and without a word she went to the bin.

"Condensed milk," she said testily.

"They'll be eating *treiffe* next," said Uncle Ike. We didn't think condensed milk was so low that it could be classed with pork or jellied eels but it didn't seem the best moment to say so. Aunt Lallie sat stroking a drooping cat.

Cousin Bernie had something in mind, as I said at the outset. We were at a bit of a loose end. At such moments we took to eating, if the adults were out, which they were. Nothing for the gourmet — bread and cheese, pickled onions, a jar of red cabbage, perhaps. If we were in luck there'd be some slices of Bloom's garlic sausage with gherkins. I was ready for feeding time.

"Wait, wait," said Bernie. "I've thought of something. You ever had ham?"

I could scent in the air conspiracy of the darkest kind. The freedoms of Aunt Lallie's house did not include crossing the line into the unclean non-kosher world.

"Ham, are you *verukt*? When would I eat ham? Ham," I warned him, "is as big a sin as bacon, you know."

Bacon we could sometimes smell tantalizingly drifting in from somewhere in that gentile street, but the *barmitzvah* boy was not going to be put off.

"You sure you've never had any?" As a matter of fact I wasn't sure. Here was that time when a little family crowd went on a paddle steamer, the Royal Sovereign, from Tower Bridge to Southend. Great-aunt Ray gave me a delicious meat sandwich, the taste of which I couldn't quite place.

"What's in Aunt Ray's sandwiches?" I asked my *booba*.

She didn't bat an eyelid and said, 'Pressed beef', which I knew wasn't true and I half-guessed that I had eaten forbidden food.

"Tell you what," said Bernie. "Let's go and buy some ham. We'll see what it's like."

If it was going to be like Aunt Ray's stuff, I was all for it. Irresistible.

"You know that little *goy* shop next to the Fire Station? I've seen it in there. Looks lovely."

We went down the road and stared into Hawking's shop like Bisto kids. You could see this magnificent ham resting on a china stand. From time to time Mr Hawking took large pink slices from it with a long steel knife. We slavered.

"Come on," said Bernie.

I was a bit nervous, perhaps, you never know, someone would see us and it would get out. But by now I was dying for one of those pink slices, *chalishing*. Bold as brass Bernie bought some ham, neatly sliced onto grease-proof paper. I was sure Mr Hawking was giving us a strange look. Couple of little Jew-boys buying ham. Very odd.

We rushed back to the house. In the kitchen Bernie opened the packet. We both looked at the ham and sniffed the air. It might have been caviar.

"How do you eat it?" said Bernie. "Do you have to cook it?" I thought he knew.

"No," I said, with the bogus confidence of the newly appointed ham expert. "It's cooked already. You make sandwiches. Ham sandwiches. That's what you do."

Bernie sliced the bread busily and I got out the butter. I began plastering a slice of bread with a thick layer of butter. Bernie stopped, knife in hand. I looked up and could see something had appalled him.

141

"Are you mad? Are you mad?" he shouted. "You're mixing *milchikke* and *fleischikke*! You mustn't do that! Ever! It's the biggest sin you can do."

I couldn't believe it. I laughed in his face.

"Ham you can eat and you won't drop dead but mixing *milchikke* and *fleischikke*..."

Bernie was hurt, I could see that. I don't know how he finally worked his way through his confusion but he wouldn't touch any of the ham, butter or no butter. I laughed again and ate the lot. In sandwiches. Yes, ham, bread and lots of butter. *Milchikke* with *fleischikke*. Lovely, they were.

The last time I saw cousin Bernie he was in a military hospital in Manchester during the war. He was recovering from TB. I took him some very fine ham sandwiches which, against the odds, I'd managed to get hold of. Don't ask how. He opened he packet and burst into laughter, as I knew or hoped he would. He opened up one sandwich carefully and looked at the buttered bread. — Milchikke with fleischikke, eh? he said. We both fell about. Then he tucked in.

Zeider and The Suit

When he was seventy-two my grandfather, my *zeider*, that is — fell down in my auntie's garden and never got up again. Poor little Helen, my cousin, ran crying for help because there was no adult in the house. I imagined him crashing heavily into the flower bed, his nicotine-stained walrus moustache burying itself among the pot marigolds and the scared bees. My cousin, showing me later, said,

"He liked those goldy ones best. I found his glasses under the leaves."

He liked dahlias, too. Why else would he have raised them in our tiny unpromising back-yard year after year, a dozen plants at most with their heavy, purplish-red blooms as big as the palm of your hand? Every autumn he lifted the tubers as carefully as a suburban gardener would and put them in the left-hand drawer of the kitchen dresser. I used to sneak a look at them from time to time and wonder how these grimy bunches of little potatoes would throw up strong shoots and produce flowers. When the milkman's or coalman's horse obliged I would dash out with the fire-side coal shovel and a stick to collect the steaming dung. Another miracle: horse-poo was going to provoke the opening-out of those multi-petalled flower-heads.

Why did he grow nothing but dahlias? More to the point, where did he learn to do it? And where did he get his first tubers from? I invented a gift from one of his *chaveirim* at the Tailors and Garment Workers Union club in Ford Square. A little brown paper bag was handed over like contraband and the occult mysteries of dahlia culture handed over, too. Pure invention, of course. I couldn't imagine that Zeider had brought gardening know-how from the muddy alley of a *shtetl* in Poland. Yet only a few days ago I read a poem, a sentimental hymn to the archetypal *shtetl* where there were,

"...old Jews in orchards in the shade of cherry
trees"

On the other hand, Isaac Babel tells us that, when he
played truant from his violin lessons and wandered out of
the Odessa ghetto into the docks, a sailor who befriended
him discovered he wanted to be a writer but didn't know
the names of common trees and birds. 'You can't be a
writer,' he told him, 'if you don't know the names of the
trees and the birds.' I think Zeider was more like Babel
than old Jews with their orchards and cherry trees.

Why did he grow nothing but dahlias? Why not
marigolds, for instance? My sister Sylvia said he helped
her grow pansies from a packet of seeds. Nothing in my
memory delivers anything other than his lonely dahlias.
Indeed, as I remember it, in the Jewish East End no one
knew the names of the trees and the birds. It was a flow-
erless world. I cannot recall a flower shop in the Commercial Road or the Whitechapel Road. I can't recall a flower
stall in Hessel Street Market wedged in amongst the barrels of pickled herring, *heimisha* cucumbers and sacks of
bagels. I can't find in my images of the jostle of Petticoat
Lane, with its *schleppers* and barkers, a single bunch of
flowers. There were no vases of flowers on front room
tables nor amidst the biscuit barrels, brass candlesticks
and silver *menorrahs* on sideboards. Sylvia said flowers
were for hospital visits and you could buy a bunch from a
kind of kiosk outside the London Hospital. Yes, and there
were white carnations in men's lapels at weddings, a con-
cession to anglo wedding regalia. If I had thought about
that at all, and I don't think I did, I would have attributed
it to benighted immigrant-ness like the weird mixture of
English and Yiddish or the inability to understand why
their teenage children wanted to go camping in muddy
fields with only a bit of white *schmutter* over their heads.
Liegen afen drerd, they would say, lie on the ground when
you've got a warm bed with a *daunendecker*? Only for
madmen and poor tramps. In one night you could catch

144

your death. Zeider's dahlias were in a small way an act of defiance, a rejection of the old taboos and fears.

So I've decided he was a town Jew not a *shtetl* Jew. Not from Kratchikrak, that impoverished spot in folk legend, but from Warsaw, perhaps or Lvov or even scholarly Vilna. Back then I hadn't an inkling of what bit of the map he had emerged from to take a long-distance train and a North Sea boat and deliver himself to a lifetime bent over a sewing machine, working the treadle and pushing a million yards of cloth into the rag trade. I never once asked him, Zeider, where do you come from? Show me on the map. And tell me about your mother and father. Have you got any brothers and sisters? But at the time they weren't my kind of question. Anyway, my *zeider's* earlier life had gone missing. He seemed unencumbered with a pre-marriage past. No relative, close or distant, ever turned up at the street door or sent a letter. To me it was all the more strange because my *booba's* past was a fat story book in which there appeared every grade of kinship extending to in-laws of all sorts, cousins, first, second and beyond, greats, great-greats into the distant past and there were her sisters, my great aunts Sarah, Ray and Bella, my great-grandmother Miriam who had catered for weddings and *barmitzvahs* in Newcastle. There were the gold and diamond seekers in Durban and Johannesburg whom we never saw, except for the one who arrived in a fat white car, had all the kids gawping and never came again. They all stood behind her and animated her talk, reached across the globe and back into the Nineteenth Century. But Zeider had not a single forebear. Not a single name crossed his lips not a single tale about one. So how would I know where his dahlias came from? Or, come to that, what were the beginnings of his talk about class struggle and the dictatorship of the proletariat?

It's not as though he was a taciturn man and I had reason to know. I spent a lot of time with him and it always bubbled with talk which I treasured. We went out together. He took me to play clumsy two-man football in

145

Victoria Park. Anyone could see he hadn't an idea of how to kick a ball and his legs were already giving him trouble. Near the park gate was a little dairy where we had a glass of milk and a huge biscuit. I went with him to the Yiddish Theatre to watch Shakespeare. It was Macbeth which he know I'd done at school. We went up the Mile End Waste together and fingered junk on the stalls. Sometimes he'd get me weighed on a huge balance with a chair on one side and weights on the other. We ended up having sarsparilla from a barrel surrounded with ice. We went to Speakers' Corner in Hyde Park with its bizarre collection of orators and ritualized heckling. Only when I got a bit older did I realise it was an entertainment, street theatre spiced with politics. It was always followed by tea and pastries at Marble Arch Corner House where he patiently explained the speakers' jokes and obscure debates. Why, for instance, did a heckler keep shouting out, What was the role of Borodin in the Chinese Revolution?

A regular trip was to the Tower of London gardens to admire the famous dahlia border. I too was dazzled by it. It was several yards deep and about fifty yards long. The dahlias from the huge cactus sort to the little pom-poms were graded from front to back.

"Such a sight," he said "*es geht in aller glieder* — it flows through all your limbs."

He'd stand and breathe in deeply as though he could inhale all his pleasure and hold it inside himself. The border rang along the edge of the huge moat which ran round the grey stones of the Tower. We'd turn and watch a phalanx of soldiers marching meaninglessly to and fro. A sergeant was barking orders. The moment one order was given it was followed by a different one.

"What are they doing that for?" I asked.

"For nothing. It's pack drill. Punishments. With armies, is always punishments. *Oi*, armies. We shouldn't know of such things."

"What are they punishing them for?"

146

"Breathing, or laughing, mebbe." We turned back to his adored dahlias.

There were four of us kids in the house — me, my sister and two cousins. Zeider singled me out to be his Reader as someone else might be appointed an amanuensis. I'm not sure why unless it was because my mother, the eldest of his six daughters, was his favourite. They marched in demos together, went to rallies which they talked about for days and they spent hours together planning The Revolution. As a seven-year-old I stood between the two of them, holding their hands during the General Strike of 1926, watching grimly the troops and armoured cars going down the Commercial Road on the way to the Docks. The bond between them must have begun long before they worked together to topple The State. The story goes that my mother taught him to read and write English when she was a very little girl. My Aunt Lallie liked to tell it as though she'd been there. It worked like this. When my mother was learning to read and write at school at about four or five years old, she came home each day and gave Zeider a version of what she'd learned. The fact that he was literate in Hebrew and Yiddish would have helped, of course, but it must have been tough going because he was still learning to speak English. For how long this went on nobody said but eventually it did the trick. To this day I am deeply moved by the picture I construct of the little girl coaching her father and his ready acceptance of being for once the taught rather than the teacher. Far from being a humiliation it must have filled him with pride and love. No wonder they became good comrades.

So it came about that my *zeider* could eventually read English and I rejoiced in it all those years later just as I did in the fact that he didn't have a straggle beard of wire wool, go around with his head covered all the time, nor spend hours rocking to and fro at his prayers. I see him seated among his heraldic dahlias with his *Daily Worker* almost at arms-length, specs at the end of his nose, lips moving. And not just the *Daily Worker* but also *Plebs* and

147

Labour Monthly. He would get tired, though, or perhaps he just liked being read to, re-living all those hours of apprenticeship. That's where I came in.

"*Boychik*," he would say, "*sei a mensch*. Read me a *bissel*. Here, this. The bit about the Polikoff strike. You know Polikoff's, that barrack in Curtain Road. Old Polikoff, the *momser*, wants to cut their wages. Read. Read."

So I read, ploughing through the indignation of the *Daily Worker* and beginning to assemble the glossary which I came to assume was obligatory — solidarity, scabs, picket lines. There was also a blurred photograph of the picket line and you would make out in it some mounted police.

"See, a capitalist boss is a capitalist boss. The leopard can't change its spots. Old Lipschitz over the road thinks because Polikoff is a *yiddel* and his workers are *yiddelech*, he'll treat them good. There's no difference. A *yiddisher* capitalist like Polikoff, the bloodsucker, or Henry Ford, the *anti-semeet*. You think there's such a thing as a *yiddisher* wage cut? See those cossacks. He stabbed at the photo. They'll always be there for the bosses. They don't inspect them first to see if they've been circumcised."

"Zeider," I said anxiously, "suppose they lose?"

He picked up his paper and specs again and looked up at the sky for a moment or two.

"On the way is a lot of defeats. We've had worse. Before 1917 was 1905."

I knew more about 1066 than 1905. I also knew when to stop questioning and leave it at that. So in my sittings as Reader-to-Zeider there was a slowly emerging and elaborate syllabus which never appeared between covers but would have made them have a fit at the Board of Education.

There drifted in and out of Zeider's talk references to all sorts of left-wing organisations, many of them long-since defunct or moribund. They were like a secret code because they occurred mostly as sets of initials — S.D.F., B.S.P., S.P.G.B., W.S.F., I.L.P. and, of course, the C.P.G.B. There was also something called the *Bund* and the Workers' Circle. Needless to say I couldn't crack this code and made very little of the bitter hatreds and acrimony which surrounded it. From the smoke of battle there emerged the banner of the Communist Party which to me was not a set of pre-1914 initials but what my mother and Zeider busied themselves with. Listening to my *zeider* I learned that his intonation alone would tell me whether a given organisation was damned beyond redemption or given the seal of approval. It was, and still is, the dialect of the Left. Up from the depths came Lucifer, the fallen angel, Trotsky. The venom injected into his name was almost frightening especially as I didn't know what he'd done to deserve it, and why he seemed so much more sinister than the Polikoffs and their like. Once Zeider slipped in the fact that before the First World War his party had been the Social Democratic Federation. The niceties of doctrinal polemic left me lost and I was amazed when he spat out the name H.M. Hyndman, an S.D.F. leader. Zeider, in a frenzy of anger, denounced him for supporting the war.

"A class traitor, I crap on him."

How could he burn on such emotion so long after the event? He might have been speaking of someone who had done him a grave injury the day before rather than an obscure time-server twenty years earlier. That was how he annotated for me the political world, complementing my mother's little lectures which were even more didactic than his.

Still, when a session was finished he'd give me a ha'penny.

"A servant I've got. Doesn't even get the rate for the job."

It was the nearest I had to having a father since my own was not about.

For all the solemnities of the class struggle he was good at laughing and would bring a very meaty fist down on the table to enjoy his own and other people's jokes. His own jokes baffled me at first and I would have to put on a phoney laugh at stories I wasn't ready for. He once told me the story of the great sage Rabbi Nachman. I've heard it in dozens of versions since. The old rabbi was on his deathbed and his devoted disciples gathered round and took their last chance to ask him the great question,

"Rabbi Nachman, tell us what is life."

They waited for a long time, fearful that they would not hear a reply. At long last the rabbi gasped out,

"Life — is like a fish."

Baffled, they hastily conferred and came back to his bedside.

"Rabbi Nachman, why is life like a fish?"

The old man looked at them.

"So — it's not like a fish."

Zeider gave the rabbi's reply the tone of impatient irritation. How was this a joke? The adults loved it. Relished it and would repeat, "So it's not like a fish" and fall about. In due course I came to laugh too. There were also his favourite bits from books he had read. He knew he spoke with a strong Jewish accent and had trouble sorting out the English spoken sounds for "w" and "v". he saw this as very funny so he loved to quote old Mr Weller in *The Pickwick Papers* or rather, his version

"Spell it with a wee, Samivil, spell it with a wee."

Then there were his practical jokes. He'd choose the most unsuspecting child in the room.

"Stand outside the door. Stand any way you like. Give a shout when you're ready and I'll tell you how you're standing."

Out the child would go and adopt the most contorted posture, arms twisted round the neck, bent double and a fearful grimace on the face.

"Ready, Zeider. How am I standing?"

"Like a bloody fool," he would shout.

And for him it was always as funny as the first time.

I warmed myself in his warmth. Booba was different. She was stern and tough. Never embraced me or kissed me, never said a warm or loving word. When I saw other *boobas* drowning their grandchildren with affection, noisily declaring their love, I was consumed with jealousy, especially as they so overflowed with love a little of it came my way. Some nosh was pressed on me, most likely almond biscuits or a slice of strudel. I was told what a nice boy I was, patted and my cheek pinched. It was only-to-be-expected *booba*-ness. That's what *boobas* did, didn't they? Why couldn't I have a real *booba*? My wife doesn't like me to speak this way of the old lady. All the cooking for a house of twelve people, the shopping, the washing. You couldn't manage it without being tough. And only just enough money to get by, if that. And didn't you say she would buy just for you pieces of expensive halibut because you didn't like the other fish? That must have been her way of saying something.

But I had my *zeider*. He believed in treats. One day he promised to take me to the *schvitzig*, the Russian steam baths in Brick Lane.

"You know what is the *schvitzig*?" I knew the building from the outside but didn't really know what went on in it. I imagined a room full of steam which didn't seem all that alluring and I also knew that by our family's standards it was not cheap and that Zeider would have to dig deep.

"Well, yes. It's a steam bath."

"Listen to him. Steam bath he says, steam bath. It's paradise. Another world."

So we set off together for paradise. And he was right. Calling it a steam bath just wouldn't do.

We entered the lobby and stripped off our clothes in a cubicle. Then we joined the other naked bodies in the first room. The steam swirled round us but I could make out a set of high marble steps. The higher you went the hotter you got and the more sweat streamed off your body.

"Good, eh?" said Zeider, to make sure I was enjoying paradise. "You get cleaner in here in ten minutes than if

151

you had ten thousand baths. Is only the beginning."

The naked men with big bellies were chattering in Yiddish, stretched out on the marble shelves. Some business deals were being done. The state of the tailoring trade was as ever being lamented and old friendships were being cemented. For a short while the tired tailors became Roman decadents while getting pinker and pinker.

We moved on to the next steam room, a replica of the first but much hotter. I was a bit scared and couldn't manage the top shelf.

"By the finish there won't be a speck of dirt left in you. Like a blessing it feels, don't it?"

And there was the rest of paradise still to come. You left the steam room and passed through a pair of cold sprays coming from the sides like a miniature car wash. Here you picked up bay tree twigs to rub yourself with.

"*Schmekt gut*, and is healthy, too. Helps my rheumatism."

He was pummelling his chest, twirling his arms and marching on the spot in the perfume of the bay leaves. From there we went into the plunge bath, alive with thrashing bodies. Supplied with huge white towels we went back to our cubicles, each of which was big enough to house a narrow couch. An attendant in a white jacket brought tea and biscuits and after that you were expected to sleep. I had not dreamt of such self-indulgence. Definitely more than a steam bath. It was very, very posh. Zeider put his head round the door.

"*Schlaf,*" he said, "*schlaf.* Sleep."

I didn't really feel like sleeping, wanting to go on being a lord, but as he stood there wrapped in his towel I dozed off. After a while we woke up, got dressed and left.

"*Nu*, what did I say? Another world."

When I got to the grammar school Zeider treated it as a personal triumph, even though it didn't seem to match his egalitarian principles.

"We made it, we made it, you *lobbus*."

He pored over my textbooks, stroked the pile of brand

new exercise books, colour-coded for each subject and looking splendid with the school's coat of arms and motto. He'd flick through the textbooks and very occasionally stop to read a sentence or two. I think he liked my Latin books best because their utter impenetrability assured him that the best of higher learning was taking place. He would watch me doing homework while he was pretending to read the paper. I knew he *kvelled*, at the sight of what he took to be scholarly activity. He once came over when I was doing some geometry. I had spread out my geometry set on the living room table — brass compass, protractor and set square. He rubbed his thumb along them.

"Lovely little tools. Like a watchmaker's."

He glanced at the very elementary work I had just done and I guessed he wanted to ask me what exactly the instruments were for and what my homework meant. I was glad when he didn't because I could not have explained. You did geometry because you did geometry.

"Tell me," he asked one day when he'd come to meet me at the school gate to take me to the pictures at the Rivoli and saw some teachers crossing the school yard in their gowns, "why do those teachers wear black cloaks, like a funeral?"

I could tell he was a bit disappointed that they didn't wear something grander and more striking.

"Zeider," I said, "it shows they've got letters after their names like Bee-Ay and Bee-Ess-See."

"Funny way to show it."

"We say it's only to keep the chalk dust off their suits."

And I didn't dare tell him that Mr Lee, the History master, used the long sleeves of his MA gown to clean the board and store chalk in. Zeider, after all, was in the tailoring and had views about clothes. It always astonished me when for weddings and the like he dug out of his wardrobe an impeccable morning suit and topper.

"You see, I'm a capitalist really. All I need is a cigar and a £ sign on my weskit and you could put me in a cartoon."

When my cousin Bernie was getting near to his *bar-*

mitzvah, he let me know, a little too smugly, I thought, that he was going to get his first long-trouser suit as was the custom. Zeider knew my nose was out of joint. He announced to me one day

"You know what. I'm going to make you a suit. Long trousers, of course."

I should have been unreservedly overjoyed but I worried how he could afford it and how a mere machinist was going to do the work of a full-blown tailor. Carefully I asked,

"Zeider, how will you do all the marking out, the cutting, basting and hand-stitching?"

"Do you think I haven't got that all worked out? We'll go down The Lane and get a really good cloth. And you're going to choose it. Trousers is easy, a weskit is easy. But like you say, a jacket is work for a master tailor. I'm going to ask Uncle Jack. He could do it with his eyes shut."

Uncle Jack was a master tailor all right. I'd seen him cutting suits, working along his careful fine chalk lines with giant shears which made a beautiful crisp krerch-krerch sound and had a bite like a long-billed bird. All very well but Uncle Jack and I had never hit it off. When I got the scholarship it was in his eyes almost an offence, for his daughter, my cousin, did not make it. Sure enough, one day soon after the suit project was announced, Zeider told me with a long face.

"Uncle Jack won't do it. Give a guess what he said. 'You ask me in the middle of the busy? If you'd asked me in the slack...' And then he says, 'You know what costs a fully tailored jacket?' Like I don't know. I could price one to a farthing."

My spirits plummeted. Come Bernie's *barmitzvah* I'd still be in shorts.

"*Kvetch nisht*," said Zeider. He shook my shoulder. "We'll go up The Lane this Sunday and buy the cloth. Remember what I said? You choose and I stay *shtumm* and we'll get the trimmings same time, buttons, lining, canvas — everything. That suit, I promised it. You'll have it, my life so sure."

154

And I did. We went up The Lane and stood before dozens of bolts of cloth on a big stall. I could see that Zeider knew the stallholder.

"For my grandson, here, Ben. So none of your left-over bits and pieces. A first class worsted."

"For such a boy," said the stallholder, "nothing but the best."

"Leave off the *schmooze*, Ben, and no fancy prices. I'm not spending hours here beating you down."

"*Tit mir a toiver*, Joe. Have I ever sold you anything which wasn't a *metzeer*? And how's that wonderful wife of yours? Such an English she speaks and walks like a queen."

"More *schmooze*. Instead take me a bit more off the price. What's the good of being *mishpucha* if we don't help each other out a bit?"

They finished their spoof haggling and I had the makings of a suit. I chose dark blue with a faint grey stripe. Soon I saw some of it gliding under the needle of Zeider's sewing machine. And the jacket? All I can tell you is that somehow the master tailoring got done and in the busy at that. Not by benign mice in a fairy tale but I guess by a *chaver* from the Tailors and Garment Workers Union. The dahlia man, perhaps?

When Bernie came round after the suit was finished and it lay in its long flat cardboard box in tissue paper, I spilled out the whole story. We were good friends and he was pleased for me.

"Put it on, put it on and I'll see if its swanky enough for my *barmitzvah*."

I got it out of its box and swiftly changed into it.

"I wish you health to wear it. You could be the *barmitzvah* boy, if you weren't too young."

I had a year to go and wasn't going to be *barmitzvahed* anyway. Those two canny atheists, my Zeider and my mother, had seen to that.

"So," said Zeider, "what did I say? A long trouser suit you said you wanted, a long trouser suit you got. Not so bad, eh? I wish you health to wear it."

There was another great treat for me coming up. Zeider was going to take me to Highbury to watch Arsenal. We never made it. Instead, I found myself in a Daimler watching the trees flash by in Epping Forest on the way to the Jewish Cemetery. My first death, my first funeral. I didn't cry. I just wondered what I'd be doing at reading time and who would take me to the *schvitzig* again and what would happen to his dahlias.

The Dinosaur and the Professor

Some little girls were making daisy chains, smiling their way amongst the gravelly graves of Russian soldiers hastily buried in the thin strip of park close by Irmgard Strasse where I had just been stationed. The graves, scattered to the point of randomness, were those of the very last casualties of the battle of Berlin. Over each was a wooden red star nailed to a short wooden stake with a name painted on it. In that first post-war late summer the paint was already flaking. The little girls danced away, carefully skirting the graves. I stopped on the path.

Frau Somebody stopped on the path beside me. Suddenly she burst out,

"Barbarians! Barbarians! No crosses. What a way to bury the dead!"

I looked at the indignant German woman. So much I might have said. About barbarians, for instance, or ways of disposing of the dead, but I took my words and my anger away with me through the once genteel suburb of Zehlendorf, past the tank turrets sunk at crossroads, taking in the acrid smell of brown coal from thousands of improvised stoves somewhere in the rubble.

Once on an overcrowded underground train (they had started up again) I stood strap-hanging and a middle-aged man, seeing my uniform, stood up and deferentially offered me his seat. He seemed baffled by my impatient refusal. The others in the carriage watched and then looked at their feet.

And then there was that day when you could feel the arrival of winter and you started turning up your great-coat collar. I stood on the platform of an underground station which took Berliners out to the woods and lakes on the edge of the city. It was crammed with people who had been collecting wood and had strapped bundles of logs and branches to their backs. The stronger ones had collected prodigious quantities which jutted above their heads. They stood there silently waiting for the train. A little old man stood near me. He was bent double under his load, his grey pointed beard stuck out in front of him. He could have been a figure from a folk story, a woodcutter returning home from fuel gathering but with one startling difference. His face was a strange yellowy-grey and his eyes were fixed in an unnatural gaze. He's going, I thought. At that moment he fell. I stepped forward and knelt beside him to unhitch his load and loosen his collar. His eyes rolled and he made a dry sound in his throat. He's finished, I was sure. Not one of the other wood-gatherers moved or looked down. And the train came in. As though we were nothing more than an obstacle, they stepped over us and crammed into the train. Twenty minutes later the two of us caught the next one for by then the old man had struggled to his feet.

Later than year the first snows came. I had found my way to Invaliden Strasse in the Russian Sector and was making my way to the *Geologische und Palaeontologische* Museum. At least that's what my memory tells me it was called. The museum, with its huge Greek-column façade and pediment, you could recognise immediately as one of those European buildings which looks like replicas of each other. It had taken some direct hits from bombs or shells but was still unmistakably what it was. All its columns were still standing but it was cocooned in silence. Not a soul was about even in Invaliden Strasse. I went slowly up the broad flight of steps, hugging my big brown paper parcel and moved through powdery snow, two inches deep perhaps, towards the great doors. There was not a footprint in the snow but chunks of masonry showed through. The Museum was defunct.

My mission with the parcel seemed so absurd, so improbable that I was inclined to turn round and make my way back to my billet. But I had a promise to keep and would at least be able to tell Nan that I had tried, even while cutting a ludicrous figure entering the dead Museum to look for Herr Professor Dietrich, an aged academic who might be anywhere in Germany or even long since dead and was certainly not going to be found in amongst the rubble and debris. Nan was the mother of David, my closest university friend, and I had over several years visited the house. His father was a university teacher, grimly dying of a brain tumour, in an armchair. In spite of this cloud the house was to me an exciting revelation. David's younger brother, later a brilliant physicist, sat like a sinister conspirator in the cellarage twiddling with his ham radio transmitter and conducting improbable conversations with fellow hams in unlikely places like Brazil and Hawaii. David himself kept snakes in cages in the garden and raved about their beauty. Of the feeding of them I will not speak. The house dazzled me with its books, Cooper's marmalade, Bath Olivers, and assorted university lefties who came there to talk soberly of the coming war or listen to classical music on the acoustic EMG gramophone. Nan herself was an historian and, despite her personal tragedy, had time to be very hospitable in her brusque way to two egocentric students. I had not met before a woman who'd been to Cambridge. What's more, that had been at the end of the First World War. One day, talking of Nazism, she told me that sometime before Hitler took over she had spent a wonderful year in Berlin perfecting her German and pursuing her abiding interest in the Peasants' War. She had lived with a family who'd been very good to her, treated her like a daughter. Herr Professor Dietrich, the head of the household, was a gentle scholarly figure who always found time to help put some polish on her German. He took her round the museum where he worked and introduced her to Käthe Kollwitz's Peasants' War drawings.

And now there was Nan's letter. There was no exchange of pleasantries; just that she'd heard I was now stationed in Berlin and she knew that the order had gone out that Allied soldiers were not to fraternise (that was the word they used) with the Germans. In particular there was a

159

ban on making gifts of any kind. Did I remember, she asked, her talking of Professor Dietrich? She would send a parcel of warm clothing directly to me. Would I seek out the old man and give it to him. There was just a chance that I might find him in the Museum. Unlikely, she knew, but I must try.

Had she gone off her rocker, I wondered. She must have seen the newsreels of devastated Berlin. And what had the Professor been up to during the war? All the same, wasn't it just like Nan to send that parcel in defiance of official-dom and against all the odds to hope it would reach him. It was all of a piece with her collecting for an ambulance for the Republican side in the Spanish civil war and run-ning concerts for Basque orphan children.

Had the request come from anyone else I might have demurred. At the very least I might have checked out Pro-fessor Dietrich first. When the parcel arrived, in spite of some inner truculence, I set out for the Museum. A life-time of film watching has made me see these moments as the opening shots of a continental film — the battered Museum, the muffling layer of snow, the solitary uni-formed figure ascending the stops clutching a shapeless parcel tied with string. Who is he? Where is everybody? What's in the parcel? When is this? Where is this? Does the body-language suggest reluctance? And the building; was it a college? A seat of government? *Rathaus*? Museum? Will the young soldier go in or turn back?

No, I didn't turn back but went up to the big doors, pushed and entered what was a great exhibition hall. In the midst, defying probability, stood a vast, heroic dinosaur, its length stretching from one end to the other. The glass roof dome over it had shattered and scattered thousands of pieces of broken glass around its feet, min-gling with the snow which had drifted in. Its head still craned forward but its vertebrae had collapsed and littered the ground beneath. I thought of its sibling in the Natural History Museum in London, still intact and with which I had been on friendly terms since childhood. The Germans

160

in their miseries were still not ready to do the housework, sweep up and ready the poor dinosaur for restoration. Maybe the Professor somewhere was planning to collect the vertebrae into a neat pile, number them, protect them under sheeting and submit a meticulous report on work in progress. Meanwhile the broken-backed creature towered over me and I picked my way around it and headed for a staircase at the end of the hall. I wasn't quite sure why I was doing that. I went up the stairs, turned at a landing and was suddenly confronted by a huge grinning gorilla. I confess it terrified me, for by now I was taut in every nerve. Then I realised that the gorilla's glass case had been blasted away, leaving him standing there like a living creature shouting 'I've survived! I've survived!'

The staircase continued but suddenly came to a jagged end, jutting out into empty air. I turned and descended warily and, as I did so, I heard, or thought I heard, sounds coming from somewhere, scrapings, a muffled thump or two, a door closing and even voices — nothing very distinct but the subdued signals of human presence. That film again. I was assembling a soundtrack. All imagination. I listened intently nonetheless, and it seemed to me then beyond doubt that the sounds were coming from somewhere deep in the basement. From the ground floor there was another staircase going downwards. I followed it. At the bottom there was a row of dim light bulbs burning which showed a long vaulted passage. Slowly I realized that all along one side was an improvised plywood partition and in it, at regular intervals, doors with numbers and labels on them. I moved along the tidy debris-free passage and started to read the labels. They told me one thing: scholarship had survived in the catacombs. The dinosaur might be terribly maimed but the lectors, the *dozents* and the professors were still in business and hard at it... I remained sceptical about my mission but there it was, on a door, 'Herr Professor Hans Dietrich'. I wasn't quite ready. I hadn't fully prepared my head for this encounter. As I stopped before the door I tried to imagine

161

how I would look to the Professor in the uniform of an occupying power and with an unmilitary, inexplicable bundle under my arm. I rehearsed my opening gambits and then knocked on the door. A voice gave me permission to enter.

The Professor was seated at his desk, around him the paraphernalia of scholarship — books, files, papers, some beautiful small fossil specimens and a microscope. There was a separate pile of what looked like to me student essays. It was all cramped, gloomy and uncomfortable. Behind the Professor's head was a black framed photograph. Anyone in Europe and well beyond would have recognised it at once: an icon of our times. It was a photo of a young German officer, head and shoulders, serious face, peaked cap, immaculate tunic and all the insignia as well as, in this case, an Iron Cross at the throat. The Professor himself was as old as I thought he would be and looked very weary and apathetic. He was clearly bewildered by his visitor. He frowned and asked my business. As soon as I mentioned Nan's name he rose to his feet.

"Nan, Nan," he repeated. "I never thought to hear from her again. Especially now. A very clever young woman she was. Did she ever write her history of the Peasants' War?"

"No," I said, and provocatively took the plunge.

"She was too busy with anti-Fascist political activities."

A blatant oversimplification, in fact, but I needed the phrase at that moment. His face closed up and he looked away and said nothing. I had so far not mentioned the brown paper parcel simply because I hadn't worked out how to carry out the awkward manoeuvre of handing it to him. Meanwhile I found myself looking at that photo, the icon. The Professor swivelled and looked at it with me.

"My son," he said, struggling to speak. "You cannot know what it is like to lose a son. Very hard. Very hard."

Leave it, leave it, I thought. A man is mourning his son. But I couldn't leave it.

"No, not a son."

And I should have left it at that.

162

"Killed," he managed to get out. "A very promising bio-chemist."

Again, I thought, leave it now. But again I didn't leave it.

"Where was that?"

"On the Russian front, somewhere near Smolensk."

"A long way away, in another country," I said, "and what was he doing there?"

"Doing? Doing?" he said sternly. "His duty, what else?"

I could have told him.

"Smolensk, on the Russian front," I repeated. "Doing his duty. What else? And your famous museum is in ruins and you're down here in the cellars. And the dinosaur's back is broken."

"We shall repair it," he said with his first smile. "We must. We have our duty too. That's why I'm still here."

I picked up the brown paper bundle.

"Nan sent these warm clothes for the winter."

The Professor stood up again. I could see now how frail he was. I dropped the bundle on the table. In the shock-surprise of our encounter we had omitted some of the basic formalities.

"My name," I said, "my name is Rosen" and I left.

Upstairs I crunched past the sad dinosaur, down the steps into the Invaliden Strasse, knowing I would not return to fraternise.

The dinosaur in Berlin was, in a sense, the sibling of the dinosaur in the Natural History Museum. Copies of the original fossil were distributed to prestigious museums all over the world.

Professor Dietrich continued to work at the museum and was much honoured in the German Democratic Republic.

163